How to Invest in Your First Works of Art

A Guide for the New Collector

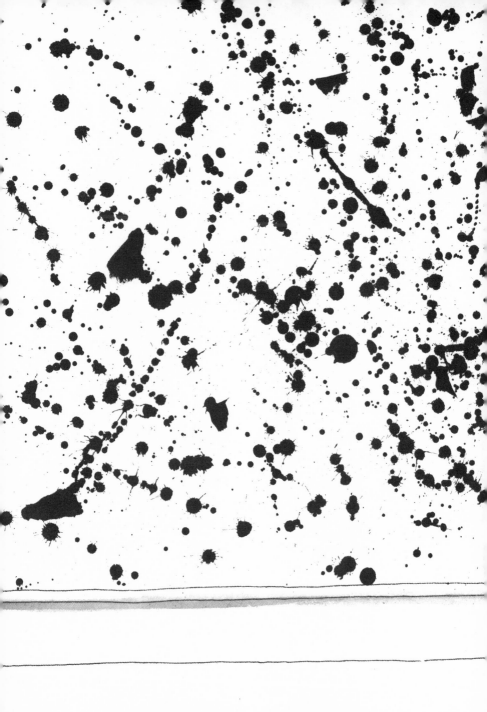

YARROW PRESS   NEW YORK   1990

How to Invest in Your First Works of Art

A Guide for the New Collector

BY JOHN CARLIN

ILLUSTRATED BY PATRICK MCDONNELL

Author's Note: Dollar figures, gallery names, and artists associated therewith are given here as of the date of publication. Such information is provided only as a general guide and not as a specific source of reference. Likewise, specific legal information with respect to conveyances, taxes, and inheritance is provided in broad generalizations. For specific advice, please consult an attorney or accountant.

Grateful acknowledgment is given to the National Endowment for the Arts and to Dodie Kazanjian for use of quoted material from *Artsreview*, "Portrait of the Artist, 1987," Vol. 4, No. 3.

Library of Congress Cataloging-in-Publication Data
Carlin, John, 1955–
    How to invest in your first works of art: a guide for the new collector/
by John Carlin; with illustrations by Patrick McDonnell.
        p.   cm.
    Includes bibliographical references.
    ISBN 1-878274-03-1 : $11.95
        1. Art—Collectors and collecting—United States.   I. Title.
N5201.C37   1990   89-29020
707'.5—dc20   CIP

Printed in the United States of America

Yarrow Press
225 Lafayette Street
New York, New York 10012

**Some are scholars, others are owners;
a great day will come when scholars
will be owners, and the owners scholars.**

—CHARLES BAUDELAIRE, 1846

CONTENTS

ACKNOWLEDGMENTS

I would like to extend my thanks to my publishers, Michael Miller and Anne Yarowsky; to Patrick McDonnell, for providing the wonderful illustrations; to the artists, art dealers, and art writers from whom I have gathered the insights and information in this book; and to my wife, Renée Dossick, for her help in shaping this book and everything else in our lives.

J. C.

1 INTRODUCTION

Over the past few decades visual artists have become media stars, and collecting art has become widespread across a broad spectrum of society. Multimillion-dollar sales of modern masterpieces have given people the impression that buying art is a great way to get rich quick. Even conservative financial consultants have concluded that fine art, on an overall basis, has outperformed most traditional investments.

Writing in *Barrons* in 1985, Barton M. Biggs, then director of worldwide research and investment strategy at Morgan Stanley & Company, concluded: ". . . a broad index of high quality art . . . has probably appreciated 9% to 10% per annum in modern times before carrying costs. This is a very good competitive return. . . . only farmland, Far Eastern equities and U.S. OTC [over the counter] stocks did better than art. . . ." At the same time, buying art can offer a level of enjoyment found lacking in most other investments. The combination of pleasure and profit has made buying art extremely attractive. Yet many people find contemporary art—now the area of greatest interest and collecting activity and therefore the primary focus of this book—difficult to understand and the traditional art markets (galleries, auction houses, expositions) hard to access and utilize to their best advantage.

This book, then, is dedicated to *demystifying* the process of buying art in order to extend the pleasure of owning art to more people and, as a result, to provide support to the artists who make it. Unfortunately, the fundamental need and desire for buying a piece of art can't be written about or taught. It is an intangible attraction that first catches your eye and then captures your imagination. First and foremost you must develop a special relationship with the artwork that makes it more than an object; that makes it something you can't or don't want to live without. As Lewis Manilow, a well-known collector of contemporary art, writes, "Why do I collect? That's really an unanswerable question. I get emotionally and intellectually involved. I look for a quickening of the blood, a pounding of the heart, and a fascination for reasons I can't explain." But apart from the purely subjective and personal side of buying art, there are many simple things to keep in mind that can help you find and afford something of value.

It is not particularly hard to list how most art professionals (i.e., writers, dealers, curators, and artists themselves) get a sense of what art is out there. In most cases a visit to one or two museum exhibitions and a stroll through a defined art gallery neighborhood will do the trick. (In New York, for example, one could visit the Whitney Museum of American Art, The Museum of Modern Art, and two of the largest concentrations of contemporary art galleries in the world, SoHo and Fifty-seventh Street, to find out what's happening.) If you do this over a period of time and read some of the glossy art magazines such as *Artforum*, *Art in America*, *Art News*, or *Flash Art*, you will begin to get an accurate sense of not only what the art world is making and selling, but what it wants you to buy.

It should come as no great surprise that the gallery world is an extremely controlled market in which monetary and artistic value frequently do not go hand in hand. For instance, if a certain young artist gets written up by an influential critic, is handled by a well-connected gallery, and is bought by wealthy, influential collectors, this artist's prices typically could remain stable even if the quality of the work does not. Why? Because the financial value of a work of art tends to become abstracted from its intrinsic artistic value. In our society more and more, art tends toward becoming a commodity, defined solely by its exchange value in the market rather than its use value as art. Whitney curator Lisa Phillips described this phenomenon as follows: "There's a clique or almost a cartel of collectors who wield tremendous influence, especially in the area of contemporary art. If they decide someone is good, then that creates an instant market among other collectors. . . ."

Taking the long view, however, the sobering fact remains that the "logic" of a market that bolsters certain prices because it is in the best interest of the few who control the market to do so, almost always fails in the long run. Often, artists ignored in their own lifetimes later become the most valuable to future generations. The most famous example of this is Vincent van Gogh, whose major paintings are now valued at twenty-five million dollars and up, but who sold only one canvas in his lifetime, despite the fact that his brother, Theo, was a highly regarded art dealer in Paris. Two lesser-known examples of this phenomenon are the nineteenth-century American painters Thomas Eakins, who sold surprisingly few of his works during his lifetime, and Winslow Homer, who supported himself in later years by running the family vacation motel in Maine. Most of his masterful paintings of the local seashore ended up hanging in the cabins as decoration. As André Emmerich, one of the most successful contemporary art dealers, recently wrote: "It is probably inevitable that the very best young painters today are being comparatively ignored, certainly by the media. It might be said that excessive publicity, especially premature hullabaloo, is likely a strong counter-indication of quality and enduring appeal."

There is some logic to the phenomenon of the neglected genius. It is not uncommon for the powerful to buy art that strokes their sense of well-being rather than art that fundamentally challenges the status quo. For instance, in the contemporary market, well-funded corporate art buyers drive up prices for work that is essentially neutral and decorative in an office context rather than for work with sexual or highly politicized content. The late Jack L. Boulton, advisor on the arts to Chase Manhattan Bank, wrote, "If I could buy Picasso's *Guernica* for five thousand dollars, it would be difficult to present that in a corporate environment. Corporations don't want distressing touches." This comment illustrates why some contemporary art that is treasured and celebrated in any given period often later serves to reflect the tastes of the buying class, rather than portray the full spectrum of the art of the period and the real value artists place in each other's work. For instance, the respected salon painters in late nineteenth-century Paris are now largely forgotten, while canvases by their less-recognized peers—Manet, Monet, Renoir, and Degas—have come to represent the age in which they lived.

With the above in mind, the new and well-educated collector should ultimately learn to rely upon his or her own sense of aesthetics and value rather than to rely on the status quo pronouncements of the day. As David Ross, director of the Institute of Contemporary Art, Boston, recently wrote, "Maybe the great painter of our time is out there living in the woods of Montana. And it will be that artist's great-grandson who will finally take those paintings in the year 2080 and show them to someone who will say: 'My God. You mean those were painted in 1986? But that changes everything we understood.' That could be happening right now. That's part of the excitement of it. It's all provisional. We could be completely wrong."

Of course you must begin by getting a sense of the art world's status quo, if only to discriminate between legitimate art galleries and mall shops that tend to reduce art to mere decoration. Basically, this book gives you the information and background you need to become comfortable with the process of buying art and understanding its financial and aesthetic value. Therefore, what follows should be used to build up the foundation of your own taste and sense of value rather than as a specific guide or tip sheet as to which artists are "hot" and what artworks you should buy.

2 THE BUSINESS OF ART/
THE ART OF BUSINESS

T he first place to begin to get a sense of what is going on in the contemporary art world and what is available to buy is by going to art galleries. They are among the best free entertainment around. Yet, for most people, walking into an art gallery can be an alienating and uncomfortable experience. Signs of social elitism linger in every detail. The message politely whispers: you are free to look around but don't bother us unless you have substantial cash to spend. There is usually little attempt to help the casual gallery-goer to understand the artist and dealer's private language. The experience is a bit like visiting a wealthy cousin's country club—it's fun to look around, but you get the sense that there is something bigger going on that you are not a part of.

Even the shape and style of the typical gallery space can be alienating. The scale and lighting are somehow wrong. It doesn't seem like those familiar interiors of home and office. Rather than being friendly and comfortable, galleries are typically cold and impersonal—places to move through, not to linger in. For most people, it is even mysterious how to behave in a gallery. Do you start to the left or the right; stare at the pieces up close or from a distance; what is the proper respect to show?

Like many American art institutions, galleries are a strange cross between churches and department stores. Everything seems to demand silence and spiritual concentration, but what it is really all about is buying and selling. To gain proper perspective, think of galleries as a bit like the Wizard of Oz. An enormous amount of energy is directed toward a certain cold and powerful image that inspires trust and confidence to attract wealthy patrons. In reality, however, behind the magnificent apparition is a person like you and me worried about meeting the next month's overhead.

It is important to keep this metaphor in mind, because the natural tendency of cliques like the vanguard art world is to make themselves appear elevated by excluding others. Yet the point is not just to peddle art to other artists, fashion designers, rock stars, and the mega-wealthy, but to build up a wide network of educated collectors.

Once you understand how to separate the hype and pretensions from the realities of the art market, you will develop an idea of whom to trust and seek out for advice. Gallery people are in many ways salespeople and therefore include the same mix of saints and sinners in their profession as everywhere else in society. To learn how to separate the two, the first thing to understand is precisely how the art business operates. For instance, what is the business deal between the artist and the gallery, and what are the formal and legal mechanics of buying and selling?

The Gallery System Ideally, the art dealer serves as a necessary intermediary between the artist and the buyer. This saves both parties the time and expense of finding and courting each other. It also saves artists from engaging in promotional and financial activities for which their temperament may not be suited. An even greater value is the psychological support that galleries often provide artists. Many of the best dealers support artists whose work does not make immediate commercial sense but who they feel are important in a greater, artistic sense. Therefore, the dealer is not just an economic broker but a supplier of a wide variety of services through which the artwork interfaces with society.

In return for such services the art dealer typically expects an exclusive right to sell the artist's work and extracts as a commission a higher percentage of the sale price than virtually any other type of agent. The universal formula is that the gallery and the artist split fifty-fifty all proceeds from the sale of art, although certain well-established artists have the bargaining power to reduce the gallery's commission. (Typical agents' commissions in other media like book publishing, music, or film run between ten and twenty percent.) Out of the artist's share comes his or her overhead: supplies, living expenses, and taxes. Out of the gallery's share comes its overhead: the rent, insurance, taxes, salaries, and the cost of advertising (duplicating costs, mailing photos, and other promotional expenses including the ubiquitous wine and cheese opening). Given the high commercial rental costs in Manhattan, a relatively new gallery must sell between fifty thousand and seventy-five thousand dollars of art every month just to break even. This bottom-line reality, of course, makes it hard for galleries to take a chance on unproven artists and causes many galleries to go bankrupt or to rely upon economic support outside sales from current exhibitions. Typically, galleries are funded by outside partners in return for a percentage of profits and a break on buying art themselves. In addition, most successful galleries derive much of their revenues from so-called back-office resales of artwork consigned to them. Resales are described in more detail in the following chapters.

The most visible galleries are those whose success has turned them into institutions. In New York, The Pace Gallery on Fifty-seventh Street or the Leo Castelli Gallery in SoHo needs not worry about breaking even because most work exhibited is already presold at prices most people cannot afford. Well-known artists like Jasper Johns or David Salle typically have waiting lists of collectors in line for the artists' next-produced works. Furthermore, the reputation of these showcase galleries ensures that at any given time there is a masterpiece or two in the back room that can be had for the price of a nice two-bedroom apartment in Manhattan. But for the typical gallery that shows the kind of art a beginning collector can approach, life is a struggle. Although it appears there are more good artists in the world than galleries to show them, it is quite difficult for a start-up gallery to develop an artist roster that combines credibility and guaranteed sales. At the same time, start-up galleries often offer excellent opportunities for the collector in that the work is typically less expensive, and most of today's "blue-chip" artists began with low-key shows in unknown galleries.

The way many people first become acquainted with art galleries is through "openings." Virtually every art exhibition begins with a public reception that anyone can attend, regardless of whether they have been invited. Most such receptions offer wine, sparkling water, and cheese to whoever attends. These openings serve two distinct purposes. On one hand they are an opportunity for the artist to celebrate the culmination of a year or two of hard work with his friends. On the other hand the opening serves the gallery by introducing the artist to potential clients and by generating word-of-mouth about the artist's work, which is often crucial to develop sales and press coverage.

For the potential collector, opening parties give a general sense of the personality and identity of the gallery in question. In a larger sense they also serve the art world by providing an opportunity for cross-fertilization among the various strata of the arts community: artists, collectors, critics, and curators. This is particularly true during periods when art movements are being born.

A recent example of the above was the short-lived, but potent, East Village art scene in New York. Owing to the decline in teaching opportunities, public funds, and the entrenchment of the SoHo gallery system, a network of artist-run galleries flourished in the Lower East Side of Manhattan between 1983 and 1987. At first rents there were cheap, and storefront spaces like the Fun Gallery and Gracie Mansion Gallery began showing relatively affordable art that expressed the sensibilities of a young generation that grew up in the sixties. Peter Nagy, an influential East Village artist who also ran the Nature Morte gallery, says, "One of the reasons all the East Village galleries happened in the early eighties is that there was a desire for the artists to have more control over the marketplace and not to be naive about the situation of an artist within the marketplace. There was a desire to take a more hands-on role with the actual display, selling, and marketing of art." Openings in the East Village often turned into de facto block parties as people spilled out of the tiny galleries and onto the streets. East Village openings were in sharp contrast to the traditional upper-crust Fifty-seventh Street art openings that were geared more to the habits and tastes of those who buy art than those who make it.

But times changed, and the success of the East Village art scene caused its own downfall. Real estate in the area suddenly became desirable. This fact drove up rents to the point where the cost of gallery space in SoHo and in the East Village became virtually the same. Also, many of the key artists left for more mainstream SoHo galleries as soon as the opportunity presented itself. Finally, most of the East Village galleries folded or pulled up their stakes and moved to SoHo, which, by the end of the eighties, had become the most consolidated art gallery neighborhood in the world. The effect of the East Village can still be felt in the art currently being produced and the overall social atmosphere of the art world as expressed in opening parties. In fact, the East Village was just the most recent in a long series of countercultural tendencies in the art world and defined one side of what could be described as the predictable pendulum swing of artistic taste between formal elegance and everyday funk.

In addition to the tone of the opening party, the identity of a particular gallery can be gleaned from the picture it creates in the mind of the public as the place to go to see one or two defined types of art. This grouping of similar kinds of art is typically referred to as the gallery's stable of artists. Some contemporary art dealers, notably, Leo Castelli and Mary Boone, have raised this concept to an art. For most of its existence the Leo Castelli Gallery has had a virtual monopoly over the artists of the Pop era—Jasper Johns, Robert Rauschenberg, Roy Lichtenstein, Andy Warhol (while he was still alive), James Rosenquist, and others. The gallery also shows key work by less celebrated artists like Bruce Nauman and Richard Artschwager, and younger artists like David Salle and the Starn Twins, in conjunction with the galleries that first brought them to the public's attention. Across West Broadway from Castelli in SoHo, Mary Boone has put together one of the most formidable stables of blue-chip eighties artists, including the Americans David Salle, Eric Fischl, Barbara Kruger, Sherrie Levine, Jean Michel Basquiat, and Julian Schnabel (who later moved uptown to The Pace Gallery), and German artists (in conjunction with the Michael Werner gallery) such as Sigmar Polke, A. R. Penck, and Jorge Immendorff. Because galleries often develop aesthetic identities (a list of prominent galleries and their "stable" of artists is set forth in the Appendix), visiting a group show, put together at virtually every gallery during the slow summer months, offers an excellent opportunity to get a sense of that identity and the range of artwork currently available at a given gallery.

One of the most mystifying aspects of the art market is how prices are set for work by young artists without established sales records. As is described throughout this book, value in art is not intrinsic in terms of either the cost of materials or the amount of labor involved. Furthermore, art is one of the least liquid (i.e., readily exchangeable) forms of investment. In other words, a work of art is only worth what someone else will pay for it. A large part of the gallery system is dedicated to balancing the uncertainty of artistic value with a clear, stable price range for a given artist. Once that artist's work is sold, every sale establishes a clear market for such work. The gallery then raises prices steadily in each of the media in which the artist works. A gallery will virtually never reduce the established price for an artist's work more than ten or twenty percent because that undermines the gallery's relation with its clients with respect to the unstated understanding that values will rise. If an artist no longer sells in an established price range, the gallery will more likely sever the relationship or continue it despite low sales rather than reduce the asking price.

The way a new artist's work is priced takes into account several factors: the scale of the work (including the cost of materials and labor involved), the reputation of the artist (how hungry collectors are for the work), and the price range for similar work by other artists. In general, few paintings or sculpture by new artists showing at established galleries sell for less than twenty-five hundred dollars or for more than ten thousand dollars (although some work by unestablished artists at new galleries or alternative spaces may be slightly less). These figures are actually quite reasonable in the context of what the artist receives relative to the time and expense he or she incurs. For example, if a painting by a respected young artist sells for six thousand dollars, the artist receives fifty percent of that amount, or three thousand dollars, from the sale (assuming there were no discounts or costs deducted from the price). Even if the artist can make and sell ten such paintings a year (unlikely for even the hardest-working artists), his or her annual income will be far below that of the average office worker. If you add to that the expense of renting a studio (an absolute necessity to create large works of art) and the cost of materials, the artist's real income is frightfully low.

The actual figure charged for the artwork in the twenty-five hundred to ten thousand dollars range is often reached in a less than scientific manner. It depends upon the dealer's instincts as much as any objective formula. In the long run, the difference between paying six thousand and eight thousand dollars will likely be immaterial. If the artist's work does not sell in the future, it will be worth less than you paid, if anything. But if the artist's work continues to sell, the dealer will likely see to it that prices steadily climb to the point where they can rise well beyond the start-up price you paid. In other words, by assuming the risk of accepting the dealer's word as to the value of an unproven work, your chances of actual gain (or, unfortunately, loss) are that much greater.

It is important to keep in mind that virtually every gallery will make art available to you upon request that is not currently on exhibition. In fact, one of the great secrets of the art world is that you can walk into a gallery and ask to see examples of any artist the gallery shows. A good place to start is to request to see the slide file for the artist in question. This will give you a good overview of the artist's career and the range of work available. These files also include press clips about the artist that can help you understand the work and assess its current reputation. Of course looking at slides in a gallery is somewhat absurd because it is the one place where you can see the work itself. Slides and other reproductions that galleries make available, like color transparencies and black-and-white glossies, should only be used to get an overview of the artist's work. The most important opportunity to capitalize upon is to have work brought out of storage for viewing. Many galleries have a back room set aside for this purpose. People often fail to take advantage of this opportunity because of the gallery's typically exclusive and intimidating atmosphere. But if you appear serious and interested, most galleries will be all too happy to cater to your request.

It is also important to keep in mind that to get the most out of a gallery you must know what to ask for in advance. In addition to the slide file and press book, ask for any available catalogues of the artist's work. Also, be sure to ask about the full range of media in which the artist works. If paintings are out of your price range or not to your taste, drawings, prints, or sculptural objects may suit your needs.

Once you have demonstrated a serious interest in an artist's work (usually by buying one or two pieces), you may be able to arrange a visit to the artist's studio to meet him or her, get a sense of the process of creation, and see work that may not yet be available to the general public.

Painting Art into a Corner: How the Dealer Deals One of the odd things about the art market anywhere you look is that it strives not to appear to be a market in the typical business sense. In fact arrangements between artists and galleries are typically oral and rely on a handshake rather than a formal contract. Because of this, particularly in New York, laws have been developed that regulate dealers to a certain extent. The most important recent regulation from the buyer's perspective requires galleries to prominently list the prices of the works exhibited. Many dealers resent this obligation, but it is obviously of great value to the buyer, who wants to know that he or she is paying what others would pay for the same object. These price lists are usually at the front desk. Of course in reality this rule can often be circumvented, for instance, by giving deep discounts to favored customers. But, in general, agreements between artists and dealers provide that galleries can only discount up to ten percent without the artist's consent. Therefore, right off the bat, everyone in the know bargains to pay ten percent less than the asking price. Galleries are often also authorized to give twenty percent trade discounts to institutions and professionals like consultants and other dealers. In rare instances, greater discounts of as much as forty percent are also offered to certain other dealers, independent consultants who have a special relationship with the gallery, and investors in the gallery. But a discount in the range of ten to twenty percent is usually the limit, and within this range, you can try to negotiate for the best price in the same way you would for any major purchase.

After reaching an acceptable price on a work of art, another point to negotiate is the payment schedule. Most galleries let buyers go "slow pay," which often means you take the work home with a one-third down payment and a guarantee of successive one-third payments over the next six to eight months. Also keep in mind, particularly when buying prints and drawings, that there may be an additional hidden charge for framing. You should always ask whether the list price includes framing, and if so, how much and whether it is obligatory. If the framing cost is too high, you might want to frame the work yourself.

The other important New York State law that impacts upon the buyer provides that if there is no agreement to the contrary, the artist has consigned rather than sold the work to the dealer. The consignment means that the dealer has certain specific fiduciary obligations to the artist. What this means in lay terms is that the dealer sells the work on behalf of the artist and owes the artist a duty of care with respect to the artwork and a duty of responsibility with respect to the financial accounting for the sale. In addition, if the gallery is declared bankrupt, the artwork cannot be sold upon liquidation because it is not owned by the gallery. Other states, particularly California, have similar laws that specifically protect the buyer and the artist from unscrupulous dealers. Outside New York and California, the most legal protection available is found in the Uniform Commercial Code (as adopted in virtually every state), which protects buyers in virtually any commercial context.

The importance to the buyer of the legal relation between artists and dealers is twofold. First, you need an accurate sense of how things work to judge your relationship to them. Second, the single most important legal question in buying art is that of title. You must be certain that the person selling the art has the right to sell it to you, because only he or she can pass along to you what he or she rightfully has in the first place. In a dispute over title, it is possible that the artist (or prior owner) may be entitled to recover the work—from you. It is generally safe to assume good title when dealing with well-known reputable galleries, but otherwise it doesn't hurt to ask. This is particularly important in the art market because of the often confusing and volatile relation between artists and dealers and the high volume of stolen art recirculated through seemingly legitimate channels. As recent news reports have demonstrated, the buyer must be particularly vigilant as to the issue of title and authenticity in buying prints by well-known artists like Salvador Dali and Marc Chagall, as discussed further below in the section on Multiple Editions. Legally, a buyer can rely on the seller's right to convey title, which means that the buyer can sue to recover the amount of money he or she paid for the artwork. But, obviously, when you buy a work of art, you hope not to get involved in a lawsuit.

It is important to keep in mind that aside from the specific New York State laws mentioned above, there is virtually no regulation or licensing of art dealers either in the United States or internationally. Therefore you are on your own and should request the following in any purchase over a few hundred dollars: (1) a warranty of title and authenticity, and (2) a certificate stating the amount paid, the name of the artist, title of the work, when the work was executed, and the materials used. A simple bill of sale from the dealer should state these items and have sufficient legal status to protect you. The certificate should be signed and dated by the dealer or, better yet, by the artist. It is also important to record the amount paid to provide a basis for capital gains tax upon selling the work (discussed further below). If you are buying work in the high end of the market, it pays to have a lawyer review the paperwork or prepare a satisfactory bill of sale. The most obvious analogy is to that of buying a house. No one buys a house without doing a title search and doing the proper paperwork. The same should hold true for any work of art that costs almost as much as a house.

Another important consideration in buying art is what exactly is being bought. This is not as simple as it might appear. Under the relatively new United States copyright law (which went into effect in 1978), the sale of an art object no longer automatically includes the copyright in that object or the image it embodies. The artist retains the copyright. What this means is that any revenues from the reproduction or commercial exploitation of the artwork flow entirely to the artist and not to the owner. For instance, if you buy a well-known painting after 1978, and postcards, posters, tee shirts, or calendars are made of it, you will not share automatically in a percentage of royalties. Such proceeds flow directly to the artist who created the painting and who still owns the copyright even if you possess the object. The law does not stop a collector from buying the copyright, but to do so a formal assignment of copyright is required that must be registered with the Copyright Office in Washington, D.C. Also, you may be expected to pay more for the work and *should* pay more if you buy the copyright along with the artwork itself.

Oddly enough, many major museums and art publishers have not taken account of this change in copyright law in their clearance procedures, and they typically secure releases from the collector and not the creator of the artwork when reproducing it for catalogues, postcards, and posters. This issue will undoubtedly become more volatile as the commercial value of art reproduction and merchandising rises. For instance, the Warhol estate recently signed a merchandising deal roughly parallel to that typically associated with the licensing of cartoon characters and fashion designers. The prospect of Warhol shops in local malls along with the already brisk business in art cards, posters, calendars, and shopping bags should make artists and collectors think more seriously about the potential revenues that can be derived from the ancillary exploitation of the work.

It is important to establish the mechanics of art commerce and to define what is actually being sold precisely because art dealers are unregulated. This does not mean they are unscrupulous. Yet people become art dealers for a variety of reasons besides the basic qualifications in business or art history. Dealing is one of the last self-made businesses, and because of this rough-hewn laissez-faire atmosphere, the buyer must beware. *Caveat emptor* is the rule when considering any art purchase.

The best dealers know how to nurture their collectors as much as their artists, so the first step is to find a trustworthy dealer who will take the time to learn your aesthetic interests and financial limits. It would be unfair to recommend actual dealers, but there are some basics to keep in mind that apply to virtually any collector-dealer relationship. First and foremost is word of mouth. A dealer's reputation is his or her lifeblood. Ask around and find one who is both knowledgeable and approachable. If you personally don't know anyone to ask, you can ask other dealers, or even call or write a local curator or art critic to ask his or her opinion. With a personal art consultant as opposed to gallery dealers, you can ask for references and call other clients to assess their opinion of the consultant and how the relationship has worked for them. In general, it always works when you find a dealer who demonstrates a true love of art, supports quality artists over time regardless of their sales, and who expresses a genuine desire to explain the artwork to you.

Most important, you must go out and test the waters for yourself. Rosamund Felsen, a well-known dealer in Los Angeles, writes, "Collectors are beginning to learn that becoming knowledgeable in the field of contemporary art requires work and time, and it is not like going out and selecting household furnishings. The better collectors are thrilled that there is a whole new world out there for them to learn and read about. . . ." Once you have thought through the issues of what artists to buy and what medium suits your needs (discussed in detail below), approach that artist's dealer and get a sense of his or her helpfulness. Usually, you will be pleasantly surprised at how accommodating a dealer will be. Often the cold facade is the inevitable outgrowth of someone who provides a free public service at great personal expense and must greet every visitor as well as every hopeful artist who comes in with a sheet of slides. After all, it *is* a business, and, if you show genuine interest, most dealers (or their assistants) will take the time to familiarize you with the artist's work and suggest work by other artists you might find of interest. As discussed above, most galleries will show you examples of an artistic work in storage, slides of older work, and press clippings upon request. The signs to watch for in appraising the integrity of a dealer is the degree to which the dealer responds to your interests rather than tries to push you into something more expensive or of more dubious quality than you want. An even better sign of a trustworthy dealer is one who discourages you from making a hasty purchase and seems more interested in developing a long-term relationship with you than in making a quick sale.

Of course, to take full advantage of the system, you have to play by the rules, the most important of which is not to try to go behind the dealer's back and buy the work at discount from the artist. Regardless of whether artist and dealer have a written agreement (usually entitling the dealer to a commission from all sales of the artist's work, through the dealer's efforts or otherwise), studio sales are a no-no. Provided, however, that if an artist is unrepresented, buying art directly from him or her is a good opportunity to get value for your money. Yet the financial risks are far greater in buying from unrepresented artists because in essence the dealer works for the buyer in establishing and maintaining the prices paid for an artist's work.

Last, consider two instances in which a dealer's integrity and a buyer's diligence can be stretched to their limits. The first is whether it matters if an artist personally executes the artwork in question. Andy Warhol made it a part of his conceptual program to remind people that he didn't actually paint his paintings. They were executed by assistants (notably, Gerard Malanga in the sixties and Ronnie Cutrone in the seventies) who often helped come up with the ideas as well. It is well known that many Old Masters made extensive use of assistants to create the volume of work demanded by their wealthy patrons. Nevertheless, most people assume that art embodies the labor and direct application of the artist's hand. They assume that part of the magic and the price is that the surface contains a permanent record of the presence of the artists themselves. The larger theoretical question as to whether it matters if a particular drip was done by Jackson Pollock or a benday dot painted by Roy Lichtenstein is beyond the scope of this book, but when considering a purchase you should ask. In some instances it may seriously affect the future value of the work unless "product" is the overt message, as with Warhol. In fact, even with Warhol, the early painted work is considered far more valuable than the later "conceptual" assisted work.

The second point that often stretches the integrity of both artist and dealer has to do with the quality of the material from which the art is made. When you buy a work of art you naturally expect that it will last longer than you will. But a large percentage of modern art, even at the very highest level, is literally crumbling before our eyes. For instance, Pollock worked with inexpensive house paint. And if you look at the floor beneath his work in museums, you will often see a pile of flakes that the painting has shed. Pollock's peer Willem de Kooning is known to have had such a penchant for rich glossy textures that he mixed mayonnaise into his oils. Unfortunately, this has proved to be chemically unstable, and the colors in his early works have been changing in a manner the artist most likely did not intend. Despite unfortunate results such as these that occur when unusual mediums are used, the work of these masters of modern art has continued to rise in value and will no doubt continue to do so unless the work deteriorates to such an extent that it is no longer recognizable.

Auction Houses   In addition to the gallery market, another important way to buy contemporary art is through the auction houses, where art with an established reputation is resold in a bidding situation that ideally raises prices. The most famous auction houses are Sotheby's and Christie's. Their multimillion-dollar sales of Impressionist and Modernist works, such as the record

fifty-four million dollars paid for Van Gogh's *Irises* and the seventeen million dollars S. I. Newhouse, Jr., paid for Jasper Johns's *False Start* (briefly a record amount paid for any work by a living artist until an early De Kooning painting was sold for over twenty million dollars less than a year later), have been well-publicized of late. But the auction houses also sell art that may be in the range of the beginning collector. According to Christie's, the average price paid for works auctioned at their house in 1988 was thirteen thousand dollars.

It costs nothing for the interested buyer to view the works to be auctioned or to attend the auction, and typically handsome catalogues are published at affordable prices. So it may be worth your while to take a look and decide for yourself if you can afford the often addictive habit of bidding on art. Auction announcements are listed in the major newspapers or can be gotten by calling or visiting the auction houses. For a particularly important or popular auction it may be best to reserve a place for yourself prior to the day of the sale. If seats are not available in the main auction room, standing room and live televised hook-ups are often used at major auctions. Also keep in mind that the major New York houses have branches elsewhere in the country and that if you register in advance you can bid by telephone.

Basically, the same business concerns should be kept in mind whether buying through galleries or at auction: authenticity of title and the condition of the work. This should take the form of both a bill of sale and what is called the auction house's condition of sale, warranty, or guarantee. You should note that the typical condition of sale in an auction house is somewhat unsatisfactory from a buyer's point of view. For instance, neither Christie's nor Sotheby's warrants as to the title of a work of art and both provide that the buyer's sole remedy is the refund of the purchase price. Again, New York State law provides some guidelines with respect to dealer's warranties. The law states that any sale by an art dealer (including galleries or auction houses) to a nondealer, which includes a written representation as to authorship and title, will be considered an express warranty and a basis upon which the buyer relied in making the purchase. These warranties cannot be disclaimed in a general way but must be specific as to a single work of art. Unfortunately this law does not apply to auctions held outside of New York, and buyers must rely upon the generally less potent provisions of the Uniform Commercial Code, at least in the United States, to protect themselves against unscrupulous dealers. But New York courts have held that New York law will apply to nonresidents who bid on or purchase art through local auctions.

The fundamental concepts that one needs to know before bidding on art through auction are those of the reserve price and the integrity of the bidding process. The reserve price is the bottom amount at which a work will be sold. Suppose you have a drawing by a well-known artist you want to sell. You take it to the head of the contemporary art department at the auction house, and if the house decides to take it on, it agrees not to sell it for less than the price you set. Therefore, if no one bids above that price it goes back to you. This is referred to as being "bought in" by the seller. Most auction houses charge a five percent fee based upon the reserve or the last independent bid and a minimum handling charge (currently around a hundred dollars) if the work does not sell. The seller also pays a fee to have the work illustrated in the auction catalogue. Color illustrations now cost approximately eight hundred dollars apiece, and black-and-white illustrations run fifty to a hundred dollars, depending upon size.

Now, suppose you are the buyer. The first thing you must do to bid at auction is to register. One does so by showing identification and signing in. Often, one must also provide evidence of credit if you haven't bid before at the auction house. Your next concern is whether or not you will be manipulated into paying more than is prudent. This obviously is the whole point of the bidding frenzy from the auctioneer's point of view. Therefore you must set your own equivalent of a ceiling before you start so you don't get distracted by a bidding war. One must hope that at reputable auction houses you don't have to worry about fake bidding, called using a shill, to stimulate price hikes. But you should be aware that some professionals often use various methods to manipulate prices outside the ordinary individual's control. One well-known example is called the dealer's ring, which is a conspiracy on the part of other potential buyers to control prices. One way in which this may occur is that professional dealers band together so that one dealer finds little or no competition on a low bid. The dealer then in effect auctions the piece to his clients and splits the profits with other dealers in the ring.

Another point to keep in mind is that people outside the auction house, on the phone or by advance written order, may be bidding against you. Finally, it is common practice for the auction house to take ten percent out of both ends of the sale (from the seller and the buyer, referred to as the "buyer's premium"). Therefore, the purchase price includes a twenty percent commission unlike the fifty percent charged by galleries. The seller's commission often rises above twenty percent if the work is sold for less than five thousand dollars. Typically, commissions charged to sellers are twenty percent for work under a thousand dollars and fifteen percent in the thousand to five thousand dollars range. When gallery dealers resell the kind of art typically sold at auction, they take less than the fifty percent commission they charge for selling work by gallery artists, usually from ten to thirty-five percent, in inverse proportion to the value of the artwork in question.

Consultants In addition to commercial art galleries and auction houses there are two other common ways for you to purchase art: through independent art consultants and at art expositions. Consultants are generally freelance art advisors who save you some of the labor of seeking out art that suits your taste in return for a fee and/or a commission. A reliable consultant also gives you someone to rely on for entry into the right art circles and to guide you through the mechanics of buying art that have been described in this book. In general it is more difficult to find a consultant than to visit a variety of galleries yourself. Similarly, a good part of the fun and experience of buying art is the thrill of personal discovery. Still, consultants are often worth their expense because they are typically not connected to any particular artist or sale as are galleries and auction houses and therefore, ideally, consultants will give you a more complete and unbiased view of what to buy. Of course, consultants are also valuable in terms of saving you a great deal of legwork and in helping you focus and develop your appreciation of art.

As compensation for such services consultants are paid in a variety of ways. On the highest level, corporations or wealthy collectors have consultants on salary who work for them over a period of time to create collections of work. On a more typical level, consultants work on a freelance basis, according to the collector's individual needs. This can range from locating a particular piece of art to assembling a range of work in a given area from which the collector can make the final selections. Freelance consultants usually take a commission based on a percentage of the purchase price of any given work of art. Such percentages typically run from ten to thirty-five percent, depending upon the work involved and whether or not the consultants' out-of-pocket expenses are billed separately. In addition, some consultants charge a flat fee or require a retainer before working on your behalf. A retainer is typically offset against the ultimate commission, but you should ascertain whether or not this is true before you enter into any relationship with a consultant.

Consultants can also be useful in selling work you already own. Overall, consultants make their living by being plugged into the market in a more direct and professional manner than most collectors can be. Therefore these consultants usually have a better sense of what is out there and who may be willing to buy or sell a particular piece of art. Consultants also often enjoy greater discounts in buying art from galleries than anyone else. These discounts can run as deep as forty percent; therefore, as a buyer, you should make sure to ask the consultant the price they paid for the work on your behalf, rather than the price listed by the gallery. It is important to calculate where the difference between a forty percent and a ten percent discount goes in terms of the overall purchase of a work and the payment of the consultant's commission. Another point to keep in mind is that some consultants actually represent artists on an exclusive basis and therefore may be somewhat biased in terms of their suggestions.

Finally, consultants are completely unregulated with respect to any legal and business standards. This is not to say that they are unscrupulous, but that you must take care to assure yourself that all the paperwork, particularly transfers of money and title to the artwork, is handled properly.

Art Expositions Art expositions are becoming an increasingly popular way to exhibit and see art in this country. The idea behind such expositions is to bring together a broad spectrum of galleries in a single place once or more a year to give art buyers easy access to the widest range of art possible. The galleries who participate in the expositions or fairs pay an exhibition fee for which they receive a designated area in which to hang work by the artists they represent. Visitors usually pay an entry fee that allows them to browse through a universe of art in an afternoon. Included in the entrance price, or for an additional fee, one can often pick up a catalogue for the exposition, which can be a useful compilation of paid ads from each gallery setting forth the art and the artists it is promoting.

These expositions vary as widely in quality as any aspect of the art world. They range from decorator art fairs to shows of museum-quality art. Expositions obviously make the most sense in areas of the country where it's difficult to see a variety of art. Yet, even in New York or Paris, such expositions have value in terms of bringing out-of-town galleries into town for easy access.

The most famous and successful of such expositions in the United States has been the Chicago Art Exposition, held each year on an enormous pier jutting out into Lake Michigan. This exposition has become something of an institution not only for Chicago residents but also for professionals in the international art market as one of the key conventions in the field. Thus these expositions not only serve the public, but also art professionals who meet at the expositions and exchange ideas and information that help set the tone of the art market in the months to come.

In general, then, galleries remain the best place to start buying contemporary art, with auction houses providing a convenient way to sell art later or to begin to acquire more established art. However, there are opportunities that exist for the aggressive collector beyond the obvious gallery and auction markets as discussed below.

Self-Reliance: There are a wide variety of alternatives for
Alternative finding and buying art, which, depending
Ways to Find upon your taste and willingness to devote
Art the extra time and energy, can be rewarding. Basically these alternatives are the ways in which art dealers themselves find the new talent they want to show. Therefore, if you trust your own taste, you can scout around for next year's new artists as effectively as dealers can themselves. Of course, in return for the extra effort and added risk you will often be able to find the best bargains around. Douglas Cramer, producer of "Dynasty" and one of the foremost collectors of contemporary art, describes that "one of the most important ways I learn about new artists is word of mouth. Those extraordinary jungle drums beat as one collector after another finds artists who are just beginning to be represented, usually in galleries that are more or less out of our normal range."

The most visible of these alternative spaces are noncommercial galleries across the country, often funded by local governments. These galleries typically run shows throughout the year that exhibit work of artists who do not yet fit into established molds. Some of these galleries, such as Artists Space in Manhattan, also have slide files that provide a vast and informative pool of information regarding artists who are not affiliated with commercial art galleries. In addition, many of these alternative spaces, such as P.S. 1 in Long Island City, New York, and The Clocktower in Manhattan, also have studio spaces that are open to the public several times a year. If you call these organizations and ask for an invitation, they will gladly oblige you.

Along the same lines, graduate art schools and independent study programs like the one run by the Whitney Museum in lower Manhattan, have group exhibitions and open-house studio visits that can give you an excellent sense of what may be bubbling up into the mainstream in the years to come. Of course the majority of student work is not fully mature and, by being derivative, often illustrates who the most influential artists are in any given moment, rather than who may be next year's stars. Yet there have been several instances over the past decade when an artist has leaped from art school to mainstream gallery success in a matter of a year or two. Keith Haring and Kenny Scharf are two recent examples.

In general these alternative spaces are best explored to take the temperature of the vibrant noncommercial aspect of the art world rather than to find things to buy. At the same time these galleries clearly support the artists who need it the most, and if you find something you like, and it satisfies certain minimum criteria in terms of execution, it will certainly be among the most affordable art available.

Finally, often at Christmastime, galleries run group shows or charitable auction shows that exhibit more modestly priced work. A few years ago the artists' collectives COLAB and Fashion Moda in New York sponsored a series of Christmas gift shows called "A More Store," where one could buy excellent signed multiples and originals for less than the typical token gift at Macy's or Bloomingdale's. Unfortunately, these gift shows no longer exist, but some similar works can be found at Printed Matter, a wonderful clearinghouse in lower Manhattan for one-of-a-kind or limited edition books crafted by artists, and which also has a large mail-order catalogue available. Also, many institutions (notably, Artists Space and the New Museum of Contemporary Art in New York, and the Walker Art Center in Minneapolis) offer limited editions donated to them by well-known artists for sale. Typically the prices are relatively low and tax deductible.

Other similar opportunities for buying art exist by looking outside the gallery circuit for artists whose work you may admire but which does not fit within currently accepted notions of fine art—i.e., work by animators, cartoonists, graphic artists, and craftspeople. Their work often offers wonderful opportunities to buy affordable objects with nowhere to go but up in value. One-of-a-kind furniture, print graphics, and original comic and animation drawings have typically been of little value because of their association with the worlds of commercial or craft art. Typically, such work becomes valuable only relative to its scarcity rather than its intrinsic quality or artistic character. Still, drawings by independent animators such as Robert Breer, Sally Cruikshank, Sandy Moore, or Suzan Pitt, and underground cartoonists such as those who publish in RAW magazine (Art Spiegelman, Charles Burns, Mark Beyer, Jerry Moriarty, Gary Panter, Kaz, Joost Swarte, to name a few), may well be among the best art values around. This also holds true for work from earlier in the twentieth century by so-called commercial artists. Advertising art, posters, and commercial photography by certain influential figures are currently highly respected from both a financial and aesthetic perspective. In addition, drawings by great comic-strip artists like George Herriman (creator of Krazy Kat) and E. C. Segar (Popeye) or animation cels (paintings on plastic film) by the Disney Studio have developed an established value in the art market. Drawings by many of their contemporaries can still be had at incredibly low prices (i.e., less than a thousand dollars). The bottom line, as discussed further below, is that value in contemporary art is really up for grabs. Part of the fun is buying not just what is considered "good" but also those diamonds in the rough that someday may become the most treasured jewels of all.

3 THE MEDIUM IS NOT THE MESSAGE

Now that you know the basic structure of the market-place, you need to know more about the content of the art itself. But before delving into the highly subjective issue of what kind of art to buy and why, a brief overview of the available media and their relative advantages and disadvantages is in order.

The first thing to mention is that American art over the past quarter century has involved rapid experimentation with new media, much of which is either deliberately in a form that cannot be sold like a commodity or involves a certain scale or mass that makes it impossible for anyone other than institutions to own and install. For example, three of the most fascinating and important art movements in recent times are Earth Works, Video Art, and Performance Art. Unfortunately, you cannot buy works in these media as you can traditional painting and sculpture. You can visit the typically enormous site-specific sculptures called Earth Works, many of which can be found in unpopulated areas and in deserts, attend a performance in a downtown theater or nightclub, or buy a videotape from certain galleries, museums, or collective distribution services like that provided by The Art Institute of Chicago; but in these three areas of art-making, the sense of collecting and owning art objects is either deliberately or inadvertently precluded. Oftentimes, artists in these or related media create objects to sell that memorialize if not embody the work because otherwise it is very hard to earn a living, and the artist is entirely dependent on institutional, corporate, or government funding.

The environmental artist Christo provides a case in point. Christo's artwork consists of well-publicized projects in which he manipulates the environment by wrapping specially made fabrics over and around well-known sites such as the Pont-Neuf in Paris or the Biscayne Bay islands in the harbor off Miami Beach. These projects involve large outlays of capital that are raised by selling drawings and studies of the project, almost like selling bonds to finance a public works project. The work exists temporarily in the real world, but you can buy expensive souvenirs of it signed by the artist. Using the term souvenir is meant only to suggest that these works are calculated commercial objects that stand in for or conjure up something else outside themselves. In effect, this holds true for much conceptual art, as discussed in more detail below.

The traditional art media consist of paintings (typically on canvas); drawings (typically on paper and also including collage); prints (primarily engravings, etchings, lithographs, and silkscreens); photographs (ranging from standard black-and-white or color prints to elaborate constructions made of manipulated photographic material); and sculpture (typically in wood, stone, or cast metal but often including plastic, paper, or other modern processed materials). The flagship media, however, of the history of art from the Middle Ages through the present time are painting and sculpture. These media are the forms historians track through time to appraise identity and change in our culture. They are also the most expensive media of art to buy, and rightly so. They typically involve a tremendous amount of labor to produce and are invested by artists and viewer alike with special significance.

In discussing the various media in which art is made, it is important to keep two things in mind. First, the medium and size of a given work of art are not necessarily important in terms of its ultimate artistic or financial value. It is only important to distinguish between media in order to understand the process through which the work was made. Second, many contemporary artists mix media, which means they combine two or more of the techniques described below.

Painting
In Western art, painting is the arena in which artists make their mark, from church altars to corporate lobbies. Large dynamic paintings connote social power, prestige, and wealth due to the fact that the largest investment necessary to create paintings is the artist's own labor. The medium is perhaps the most expressive and idiosyncratic among those that have had such an effect on our culture.

The term painting encompasses the application of many different substances onto many different surfaces. In general, paint is created by mixing mineral or vegetable powder (from which the particular color or black and white shade is derived) into oil for oil paint, into water (and gum arabic) for watercolor, or into synthetic polymers for acrylics. The liquid medium serves to hold the color chemicals together and to bind them to the surface.

The traditional painting surface, canvas, is made of woven cotton or linen fabric that is often treated or primed to mitigate the actual color or texture of the canvas itself. In traditional Western painting from the Renaissance through the mid-nineteenth century, the canvas was primed with an undercoat of brown paint that gave the work a dark somber tone. One of the great technical innovations of Impressionism was painting directly on unprimed canvas, which gave the colors the bright transparency for which the Impressionists are justly celebrated. Traditionally the canvas is stretched on a wooden support called a stretcher that helps maintain a flat, smooth surface.

The other principal surfaces on which paint is applied are wood board, paper, and, to a lesser degree, metal. Of course, given the experimental aspect of contemporary art, paint has been applied to virtually every surface imaginable. Painting on wood board was most common in the pre-Renaissance era when canvas was not available in the quality and quantity necessary for fine art. Painting on paper has been part of Western art from earliest times. Today, the type of paper can vary widely from commercially available bond to specialty and handmade papers of various weights (i.e., thicknesses).

Paint can be applied to these various surfaces with a wide variety of instruments. The most traditional one is the paint brush, a stick to which bristles are attached that hold the paint until rubbed against the surface. The trace of the brush is distinctive, and the thickness and the texture of the line is dependent upon the type of brush used and the pressure the artist applies. Aside from the brush, paint can be applied by virtually any instrument imaginable, from fingertips to sponges, depending on the desired effect.

Some artists become identified by the manner in which they apply paint. In the nineteenth century, for instance, Courbet was famous for eschewing the brush entirely in favor of the pallet knife, which gives his work a rough, textured appearance. Jackson Pollock was famous for dipping sticks into cans of thin house paint, which he then moved across unstretched canvas to create his trademark drips and splatters. Fans of late-night television who are familiar with Morris Katz—"the world's fastest painter"—know that he creates images of trees, mountains, and water by blotting toilet paper soaked with paint onto the canvas. Most artists use a wide variety of instruments in any single piece of art to obtain the effects they desire. Some of the most interesting works of art are those in which the artist scratches, rubs, and marks the surface to create his or her own distinctive style.

In addition to the paint surface and instrument employed, there are a few particular techniques with which you should be familiar. The most important techniques to contrast and compare to understand their basic strengths and weaknesses are *oil painting* and *watercolor.* Oil (or its fast-drying modern version, acrylic) painting is distinguished by the thick-bodied textures it allows. The paint is literally heaped onto the surface, leaving the three-dimensional markings that trace and preserve the artist's physical presence. Part of the attraction of some artists' work, like that of Vincent van Gogh, is the sheer physicality of the paint caused by the active markings on the picture surface. Another important quality of oils and acrylics is that they allow for glazes and varnishes that can add subtle tonality to the overall image and can help preserve the work for hundreds of years.

Watercolor, by way of contrast, is a transparent medium ideally suited for fluid, layered effects. The white paper underneath the watercolor literally reflects light through the paint to create a translucent appearance. The only drawback for artists using watercolor is that it dries quickly and therefore requires a sure hand. An opaque variation upon watercolor is called gouache, which dries with a matte, rather than shiny, surface.

Other important painting media include: *casein*, in which the color chemical is mixed with a milk by-product; *tempera*, which uses egg yolk as a binder (this was a popular technique in the Middle Ages—the most well-known modern practitioner was Reginald Marsh); *encaustic*, which mixes the pigment into wax (a technique used to great effect by Jasper Johns); *fresco*, in which the painting is done onto fresh wet plaster (this was a favorite technique in the Renaissance from Botticelli through Leonardo da Vinci); *collage*, taken from the French term *papier collé*, or pasted paper, in which cut-out paper is affixed to a surface and often manipulated with other imagery or painted effects; and *pastel*, which is a type of drawing using colored chalk and charcoal.

Painting, however, is typically not the best medium in which to begin collecting. Paintings usually cost at least twenty-five hundred dollars even by unknown artists and are often large and present problems in terms of installation and storage. On the other hand, paintings offer the greatest opportunity for dramatic increases in price. It is not uncommon for prices of works by successful young painters to go from three thousand to thirty thousand dollars within just a few years. But of course, buying the work of an unknown artist with the expectation of such profits would be foolhardy.

Drawing   Drawings are often the best way to begin collecting. They cost less and are typically smaller than paintings. Therefore, they can be bought at reduced financial risk and hung comfortably in small apartments or homes. At the same time the work was made in the artist's own hand, it is one of a kind and, as such, tends to hold its value quite well. Like paintings, drawings consist of a variety of materials and techniques, ranging from pen and ink and colored pencil to elaborate works of mixed media incorporating painted elements and collage. The principal difference between painting and drawing is that the latter is largely done on paper rather than on canvas or board.

The only difficulty with drawings is that they require some care in that they cannot be exhibited in direct sunlight for any extended length of time. A good modus operandi is to go to the dealer who handles the work of an artist you like and ask if he or she has any drawings by the artist. Typically, the dealer will pull out a portfolio or a box of drawings for you to look through. Or, if there are no drawings in the gallery, you should ask if they are available. Often the dealer will go to the artist and ask him to provide some sketches or studies that may please you. The prices of drawings, except those listed as part of gallery exhibitions, are hard to evaluate. But at the same time, they offer the collector an opportunity to bargain the price down to an affordable level. Dealers will often do so, particularly if they feel they are developing a relationship with you that will lead to further sales in the future. At the time of this writing, it is still possible to find excellent drawings by respected new artists in the five hundred to one thousand dollars range.

Sculpture   Along with painting, sculpture traditionally has been considered the most important fine art medium, and like painting, sculpture actually consists of a wide variety of materials and techniques. In general, most sculpture is carved out of, modeled, cast, or constructed from one of the following materials: stone, wood, metal and/or plastic. Sculptures are typically freestanding three-dimensional objects, but they also can be constructions that hang on the wall, machines that move under their own power, or installations that encompass the space the artwork occupies. Sculpture can range from tiny precious objects to enormous constructions too large for any museum to house.

For the potential buyer, it is important to understand the medium and technique when buying sculpture in order to determine whether the piece is one of a kind or one of an edition of work. Obviously, carved, modeled, and constructed work tends to be unique, and cast work tends to be sold in multiples. In most cases, cast sculpture is, in fact, cast from carved,

modeled, or constructed originals that may be hard to distinguish from the cast objects themselves. Most of the problems that can arise from editions of sculpture are discussed below in a separate section concerning multiples in various media.

Other problems somewhat unique to large sculptural work are transportation, installation, and storage. Some modern sculpture requires the advice of a structural engineer to determine whether or not your wall or floor can hold the weight of the art object.

Another, less obvious, potential problem is properly installing and maintaining a piece of sculpture. You should make sure that the artist or a gallery representative will move the piece safely to your home and properly install it where you want it to be seen. You should also ask the gallery or artist how to dust and clean the piece, and how to replace any parts that may wear out, such as light bulbs or motors. Finally, in reaching an acceptable price for the sculpture, make certain to inquire whether such price includes transportation cost and the base on which the sculpture rests, if applicable.

Prints and Photographs

Prints are the most common way people begin buying fine art. As multiple impressions of the same image, they are produced mechanically rather than through the direct application of the artist's hand, and they typically cost less and are more available than paintings or drawings. Yet at the same time they present the greatest dangers in terms of authenticity and quality.

First, some background is in order. There are many different techniques that are lumped together under the print rubric.

Woodblock Prints In the Middle Ages, along with the invention of movable type, artists began producing woodblock prints. This was done at first to illustrate religious texts and later employed to illustrate secular subjects, often scientific treatises. Woodblock prints are relatively simple from a technical point of view. With a sharp tool, the artist cuts into the woodblock an inverse of the desired image. The block is then inked and pressed against paper as many times as desirable or possible. Color prints are created by separating each color into a separate block and then carefully registering each impression on top of each other to create the desired effect. Undoubtedly the apex of this method in terms of both technique and artistry was in eighteenth- and nineteenth-century Japan, where woodblock prints were created with remarkable detail and subtle color in large, mass-produced editions.

Engraving Shortly after the introduction of woodcut prints, the engraving process was invented. As woodcuts are printed from raised grooves along the surface, engravings, in either wood or metal plates, are made from grooves cut into the surface. These grooves are cut into the plate with a steel tool called a burin. The ink is then rubbed onto the plate and wiped off the surface leaving traces in the grooves. Next, a damp sheet of paper is placed on the plate and passed through a printing press. Engravings were a technical improvement upon woodcuts because they more readily reproduced the traces of the artist's hand across the surface, were more durable, and could produce a finer line. When a steel needle is used instead of a burin, the printed result is called a drypoint. Because the needle does not cut as deep as the burin, drypoints cannot produce large editions of identical images. Yet the drypoint allows an even finer line and more expressive technique than engraving.

Etching The next major print technique to be developed in Western art was etching. In this process, rather than drawing directly into the metal or wood plate, the metal plate is coated with wax and then drawn into with a metal point. The plate is then dipped into acid, which bites into the metal where the wax has been removed. This creates the grooves in which ink remains after the surface of the plate is wiped clean. The most famous practitioner of this method was the Dutch painter Rembrandt.

Toward the modern era as printmaking developed into a more expressive medium, artists, notably Goya, began mixing various techniques such as etching, drypoint, and aquatint to achieve the widest range of effects possible. Aquatint is a process where resin is put onto the plate before it is etched with acid, leaving a thin, washlike effect to create shadows and similar images in the print.

Lithography By the nineteenth century another medium, lithography, emerged that allowed artists to create a printed image that came as close as possible to reproducing the actual drawing process itself. Lithography was originally done on stones, but it is now also done with metal plates. Traditionally, the stone is ground to a smooth flat surface, which is then drawn on with a waxy crayon. The surface of the stone is then treated chemically to repel ink except where the lines are drawn. The stone or plate is then passed through the press to make a print. This method was particularly popular during the Impressionist era because it reproduced the sense of the artist's active markings on the surface better than the relatively stiff etching and engraving methods. In simple terms, lithography is a colorist's medium, while etching and engraving favor line drawing. Lithography returned to popularity in America over the past thirty years as artists like Robert Motherwell, Robert Rauschenberg, and Jasper Johns rediscovered the rich, expressive potential of the medium.

Silkscreen The final important type of print is the serigraph, or silkscreen, in which a screen made of silk or a synthetic substitute is either painted on or affixed with a photo emulsion. The ink is then squeezed over the screen onto the surface in successive screens for each color required. This technique was employed to great effect by the Pop artists, notably Andy Warhol, who used the process on canvas to create his best-known imagery.

A simplistic way to keep these media apart is to think of their current commercial use. Engravings are used on wedding announcements. Offset lithography is responsible for most of the photo reproductions we see in our daily lives. Silkscreens create the better quality tee shirts that teens line up for outside rock concerts.

Photography The final print medium that is so distinct as to create a medium all its own is chemical photography. Traditionally, photography was considered separate from "fine" art, but in recent years photography in the hands of artists like Cindy Sherman, William Wegman, Robert Mapplethorpe, John Baldessari, and Duane Michals has become one of the most important and valued artistic media of all. At the same time prices for more traditional photographs by artists like Edward Steichen and Walker Evans have risen astronomically. Technically, photography is simply a sophisticated print medium in which the image is reproduced analogically by focusing light through a lens onto a chemically treated plastic film rather than being created by the artist manipulating a surface with a drawing instrument. The sensitized film is then developed into a negative from which prints are produced by shining light through the negative on a photosensitive sheet of paper. The paper is treated chemically to develop the image and fix it to create a lasting, permanent picture.

In recent years, digital, as opposed to analogue, photography has become commercially available. In this new process, the image is converted into digital information by computer and then reproduced electronically. The information is then transmitted or recorded onto tape. It can also be printed by a laser jet printer that sprays ink onto paper in colors and intensities that reproduce the original subject in two dimensions. The difference between chemical and electronic photography is roughly equivalent to the difference between conventional records or tapes and compact discs.

Multiple Editions

The most important thing to keep in mind regardless of the print technique is whether the work is merely a signed reproduction of an artist's work, photographed and printed on an offset press, or work created for and in one of the print media described above. The latter are virtually always of greater value both artistically and economically. Still, some signed reproductions can be a fine addition to a start-up collection because they usually cost less and at least have value as carrying the artist's autograph.

It should also be noted that over the past quarter century, various "master" printers have become so famous that artists go out of their way to work with them, and the resulting prints become more valuable through the association. The practice of the artist working with a master printer is commonly thought to have begun with the pioneering work of Tatyana Grosman, who convinced many of the great American artists of the fifties and sixties to visit her Long Island, New York, studio, and who singlehandedly brought back the medium of lithography and

raised it, perhaps, to its highest level. The prints that Motherwell, Johns, and Rauschenberg (to name only a few) made with
the Grosman studio, ULAE, remain among the most valuable of
the modern era both because of the artists' own reputations and
the unmatched quality of the prints themselves. In recent years

other well-known print studios such as Gemini G.E.L. have come to prominence serving the lucrative print market. Therefore, the value of a print can often have as much to do with the reputation of the printer who makes the print as with that of the artist who created the image.

The other key points to keep in mind when buying prints are: (1) the size of the edition (the smaller the edition, the greater the value of each print); (2) whether or not the print is truly an original (i.e., the artist created the image on the plate, stone, or woodblock, and the finished print is approved by the artist); (3) whether or not the plate was destroyed to ensure no future editions being struck; and (4) whether or not the print is a forgery (an all-too-common practice in the print market). Of course, these points relate only to the print as a commodity. Questions of aesthetics and taste should always take precedence. If you like a particular large-edition poster by an artist rather than a limited-edition print, you should, of course, buy the poster.

The size of an edition is typically indicated by the sign of a fraction, penciled in in the lower lefthand corner of the print outside the image, in which the denominator represents the size of the edition and the numerator the particular number within that edition. If you see, for instance, $\frac{4}{50}$ on a print, it is the fourth of an edition of fifty prints. This does not mean that only fifty prints were made. Typically, a number of artists' proofs and printers' proofs are also run but not numbered. These latter prints are not supposed to be for sale on the open market, but they often find their way into the market eventually. A reputable artist/printer will dedicate no more than twenty percent of any run to proofs, although it is often difficult to determine the actual number created. Also, the number 4 does not necessarily mean that this was the fourth print that ran through the press, particularly with respect to color prints, which run through the press once for each color and often not in sequence. In other words, the numbering is often arbitrary rather than sequential; however, with black-and-white prints, the number usually indicates sequence, and lower numbers are typically considered more valuable because the plate shows less deterioration, and the ink is more richly applied.

Many states, including New York, California, and Illinois, have laws regulating the sale of fine art prints. In varying ways, these laws attempt to warrant the dealer's representation as to originality, signature, and edition. In practice there are some unscrupulous print dealers who forge signatures and create far more prints than are listed on the edition. There could be, for example, an American and a European edition of one hundred apiece. Also, some well-known artists were reputed to have signed blank sheets of paper for sizable sums of money and never bothered to look at the final prints at all. The artists whose works appear to be most susceptible to dealers' unscrupulous practices are Picasso, Dali, Miró, Chagall, and Andy Warhol (who might not even have cared since he frequently had others—notably his mother—sign his artwork anyway).

Similar problems of authenticity arise in any area in which multiples of an artwork are sold, the most notable other example being cast sculpture in which an edition of two or three is made. Recent examples of this include artist Jeff Koons's porcelain sculptures of things typically considered "bad" in our culture (like saccharine portraits of Michael Jackson with his pet chimp, Bubbles), and John Ahearn's realistic plaster casts of his neighbors in the South Bronx. The most important thing for the collector of reproductions or multiples in any medium is to ask the dealer to warrant the limited edition. With prints this can easily be demonstrated through a cancellation proof that passes the printed surface through the press one last time after it has been purposefully destroyed by the printer. This method obviously provides proof that no more images can be struck. In other instances a signed warranty by the dealer and/or artist is the best you can get.

The situation with respect to photography is even more confusing and open to unscrupulous manipulation. So-called vintage photographs are those printed by or supervised by the photographers in their lifetime. They are commonly regarded as of greater value whether or not they are signed. As with all art the economic value of photography is usually in inverse proportion to its availability—the more examples of any particular work around, the less they are apt to be worth. For instance, photogravures (i.e., specially printed reproductions of photographs from older magazines like Steiglitz's *Camera Work*) can be as valuable as many original photographs, depending upon the quality of the image and the rarity of the magazine in which it originally appeared. Conversely, editions of photographs printed after the artist's death or long after the particular image was first exhibited can often be of dubious economic value unless signed or in a limited edition. For instance, you can send away to the Library of Congress for wonderful reproductions of the work Walker Evans did for the WPA for approximately twenty-five dollars. Recent fine artists who use the photographic medium tend to follow the guidelines established for prints by listing the edition number and that of the print struck along with the artist's signature, although the original photographic negative is rarely destroyed, which means there is always the potential that additional prints can and will be struck.

The vagaries of collecting reproduced artwork is part of what makes original paintings and drawings so valuable. But of course the real value of any artwork has nothing to do with the medium, availability, or even originality. It is the power of the work to project the dreams and realities of the human imagination in such a way that it transcends the medium in which it was made.

4 OWNING ART: HOW TO PRESERVE IT, INSURE IT, SELL IT, OR GIVE IT AWAY

Collecting art is somewhat different from *buying* art. Collecting implies a buying program. It requires long-term dedication to expanding and preserving a disparate group of objects that can be thought of as forming a single collective identity. There are three basic aspects of building a collection of art that every art buyer should keep in mind.

The first is the responsibilities of ownership: installation, care (including insurance, security, and restoration), and sale or gifts to families or public museums (including the relevant tax considerations). The second is the degree to which art is treated like other forms of equity, allowing the owner to borrow against it and use it as a measure of his or her overall financial worth. The third is the thematic, formal, or spiritual relations among the various objects you own, and how to strive for and preserve those relations.

Shipping, Hanging, and Preserving Art Once you have found and bought a work of art, the next considerations are how to get it home and what to do with it there. Most galleries will arrange to have large works shipped to you. The expense for this should be considered when calculating the price for the work of art.

However, even before buying a large work of art, you should first consider whether it will fit on your wall or sit on your floor, and, perhaps most important, consider the work in the context of your overall surroundings. After all, decoration *is* an important practical consideration when buying art, which is not to say you should buy a painting whose colors match those of your couch. If you do buy more work than can be displayed at any given time, you should consider the proper way to store it. Flat files provide an excellent way to store works on paper like prints, drawings, and photographs. Before storage, the work should be matted with acid-free paper and stacked with archival tissue paper between each piece. The proper mats and supplies can be found at most full-service framing shops and artist-supply stores. Galleries and frame shops will mat the work for you but at a considerably greater cost than if you do it yourself. Therefore it may be worth the investment to buy a mat knife and paper and ask a salesperson the proper way to cut and install your own mats.

To the extent possible, excess humidity and extreme temperatures should be avoided in storing or displaying artwork. There are three important safeguards to keep in mind when displaying works on paper. First, sunlight bleaches most prints, drawings, and photographs. Direct sunlight should be avoided altogether. In addition, this type of work should not be exposed to indirect sunlight for extended periods of time, and glass that screens out harmful rays should be used when framing the work. Therefore, works on paper should be rotated between the wall and flat storage. Second, photographs cannot be framed directly against Plexiglas because the image might become glued to the plastic, destroying the piece. Finally, it is important not to place fragile works of art, particularly those on paper, in a bathroom or a kitchen, where excess humidity or cooking oils may damage the work.

Because of their size, paintings and sculpture are more difficult to store than works on paper. Fortunately, most well-painted oils and acrylics are virtually indestructible. In fact they can be lightly dusted. With respect to further maintenance, all that needs to be done is a gentle cleaning every generation or so. If you contact a local museum or gallery, they can suggest art restorers in your area that can provide such services. Serious collectors install atmospherically controlled rack storage units to hold their collections, but most people buy only what their walls can hold.

Finally, the most important aspect of owning art is displaying it to its best advantage. Obviously, hanging art in your home is as personal a decision as deciding what to buy. Still, there are some objective criteria to keep in mind. First and foremost, make sure that the piece is secure and safe. Ask the gallery or the artist how best to hang the work. In many instances, particularly with larger works, one of these sources will provide or suggest the proper hooks and wire needed for the job. You must also make sure that you hang the work with enough nails, and in the proper place in the wall, to keep it from falling. This is particularly important with respect to plasterboard walls where you need to secure the nails into cross beams or support beams to support heavy work. In general, one or two nails, properly placed, will keep most artwork secure on the wall. It is a good idea to keep a carpenter's level nearby to keep larger paintings from hanging at an angle.

Beyond the mechanics of hanging art there are the more subjective, complex, and, hopefully, pleasurable, issues of aesthetics and design. To maximize the potential of your art collection it must be installed in an intelligent and visually stimulating manner. In most instances this happens naturally as a balance between intuition and the physical limitations of your home. Some collectors like to rotate their work to keep it fresh and provocative. Others like permanent installations that allow one to grow with a particular work of art and measure its long-term potential.

Some of the most famous collectors of modern art, such as Gertrude Stein or Katherine Drier, were famous for stacking the work in a virtually indiscriminate way in their homes. Period photos of Stein's modest Parisian apartment show works by Matisse, Picasso, and Braque hugging every available piece of wall space, a far cry from the tailored aura of respect given the work in contemporary museum installations. Photos of Drier's Connecticut home offer an almost humorous mix of old-fashioned suburban charm and modern masterpieces like Du-champ's *Large Glass* and *Tu m'*, the latter of which Duchamp made on commission to fit a space above Drier's bookcase. Once you catch the art-collecting bug, it becomes hard to own only enough to hang on your living-room wall. This provides another reason why it may be a good idea to specialize your art buying to develop a collection of work that fits both your personality and the physical demands of where you live.

Insurance and Security Even a modest collection of art can become quite valuable, which means some thought must be given to security and insurance.

There are two problems in this regard — cost and effectiveness. Insurance provides only partial relief for lost or stolen art because money rarely is an adequate replacement for a unique work of art you truly love. Of course something is better than nothing, and the money can be used to buy some-thing similar. The other problem with insurance is the expense. Often, smaller works of art can be covered under a general home or apartment insurance policy if the work is scheduled on such a policy — just as one does with valuable jewelry or antiques. Larger, more expensive artwork may have to be independently insured, which can be prohibitively expensive. Insurance coverage for any work of art should be periodically updated to reflect a rise in the value of the work.

Another problem with insuring artwork is valuation. The collector may have to incur the expense of an independent appraisal to find an agreed-upon value for the work. One problem here is that art appraisal is far from scientific. The three principal professional organizations in the United States for this service are: The American Society of Appraisers, Appraisers Association of America, and The International Society of Appraisers. Some museums and galleries also provide appraisals. The only guidelines for such appraisals are published by the Internal Revenue Service (which obviously has an interest in valuation for estate and gift-tax purposes). The fact is, regardless of guidelines and professional organizations, valuation often has as much to do with the purpose of the appraisal as the intrinsic value of the work itself. In other words, appraisers often are affected by the desire of their clients to overvalue for insurance purposes or to undervalue for inheritance purposes. The other important area where appraisal comes into play is the division of property in divorce proceedings, which can get messy when couples who have amassed important collections of art break up.

Another problem with valuation in the insurance context is whether the measure is fair market value or the original cost. But of course, the biggest and most insurmountable problem is that because art is unique and nonfunctional, its true value is virtually impossible to objectively ascertain. It is almost as hard for professional appraisers as it is for the amateur collector.

Another consideration in insuring art is what kinds of losses may be excluded from your coverage. Fire and documented theft will likely be covered, but ordinary damage, or damage caused by assistants, guests, framers, restorers, or petty theft, might not be covered. Deductibles also come into play when expecting reimbursement from an insurance company for lost or damaged artwork. In other words, if your policy has a thousand-dollar deductible, and your loss is valued at twelve hundred dollars, the insurance company is only obligated to pay you two hundred dollars.

A final consideration regarding insurance is when risk of loss passes to the collector upon buying an artwork. The general rule is that when buying from a gallery, the risk is only assumed when you take possession of the work. Typically this is upon delivery to you, unless you pick up the artwork yourself. But note that if you buy work directly from an artist (who is not legally considered a merchant), the risk passes at the moment you have been given the opportunity to pick up the work. So, for example, if you visit an artist and buy a piece on the spot but don't bother having it delivered for some time, and that work is destroyed in the interim, you may not be able to make an enforceable demand to get your money back from the artist.

Typically the most important instance in which insurance comes into play is in loaning works of art for exhibition. Many collectors are reluctant to loan work because of the increased risk of damage or loss to the artwork; but at the same time, work tends to increase in value when it is exhibited and known to the public. Therefore, if you are approached to lend a piece for exhibition, you should give it serious consideration, over and above the gap it might leave on your living-room wall. Here are some of the things to keep in mind when balancing the relative risks and merits of loaning art. First, you must ascertain that the borrower is a reputable institution or gallery that will properly insure the work from pickup to return and will display and protect the work with a proper degree of respect and care. It is absolutely essential that the borrower give you a proper loan form that allows you to set the value of the work for insurance purposes and legally obligates the borrower to provide such insurance. You should also pay attention to how the work will be shipped and installed to insure the proper handling and care. Furthermore, as discussed earlier, the copyright owner of the work must consent to the public display of the work. As the artist now typically owns the copyright in the work, he or she, or the artist's estate, must consent to the exhibition even if you own the object. This is more of a concern to the borrower than the owner, but it is something you should keep in mind.

Security is of even greater concern to the lender than insurance, because it is the work you want back, not financial compensation for loss or damage. Therefore you must be careful only to loan to reputable institutions that guarantee the proper security in the form of controlled access and museum guards.

Security is also a concern when keeping art in your own home. Unfortunately, recent publicity about rising values in contemporary art has seeped into the underworld, and thieves now may abscond with your artwork along with jewelry and expensive electronic toys. Personal security systems are expensive and often ineffective. Some artwork can be bolted to the wall to deter its ready removal, and some valuable art can (and should) be stored in safety deposit boxes or bank vaults if you are away from home for extended periods. Also, art is much harder to "fence" than most stolen property because it is one of a kind and often requires detailed provenance (a list of prior owners) upon sale. IFAR, the International Foundation for Art Research, maintains a listing of stolen artwork that puts dealers and customers on guard as to what may be too good a bargain to be true.

The whole area of private ownership and public exhibition of art raises a host of theoretical issues. The most important of which is the degree to which art ownership involves a measure of social trust. The owner should enjoy the full economic benefits or losses of owning the work of art, but he or she has an obligation to the artist and the culture at large with respect to maintaining the integrity and accessibility of the artwork. In some countries, private ownership is regulated with respect to sales to foreigners. For instance, in England, any artwork whose value exceeds a certain amount of money cannot be sold out of the country without giving local art institutions the opportunity to match the amount paid for such artwork. In this country, private ownership is virtually unregulated, except to a small extent under New York and California state laws that prohibit the exhibition of altered artwork. For example, a section of a larger work or of an installation cannot be exhibited in isolation without the artist's consent or, to give another example, an offending element of an image cannot be censored or painted over. But oddly enough, although the owner of an artwork cannot alter its appearance, it can be destroyed entirely without repercussion.

Reselling Your Art   Next to deciding what to buy and how much to pay for it, the most confusing issue in owning art is how to resell it. With the exception of very well-known artists, there is no ready market for swapping or reselling art. It is not like selling a used car where one can place an ad in the paper and invite prospective buyers to take a test drive. To sell a work of art, one must venture into a seemingly nefarious network of dealers, private consultants, or auctioneers whose incentive may well be turning over a volume of art rather than getting maximum value from any individual piece. Furthermore, as discussed above, valuing art, particularly that by lesser-known artists, can be a mysterious and frustrating process. Certain well-known artists have a ready market for their work, and recent sales establish a solid sense of value. For instance, if one Van Gogh sells for thirty-five million dollars, a similar Van Gogh is not likely to sell for less. But of course the art market is as volatile as any commodities market, and fluctuations in foreign currency rates and the overall health of the international economy affect monetary value as much or more than respect for the artist or the particular work of art.

For the average beginning collector, the opportunities for resale are much more limited than most galleries, dealers, or auction houses would like to admit. This leads to a typical catch-22 situation. If the work is well known and obviously valuable, it is easy to sell, but if the work is more modest, particularly by a contemporary living artist, it can often be difficult to sell.

Essentially, the way to go about selling art is the inverse of buying it. First go to the dealer who sold you the work and ask if he or she will handle the resale. If the artist is still associated with the same gallery, this may be the easiest route. If this doesn't work, you can approach other galleries that handle similar work, auction houses that may include your work in group sales of related work, or independent dealers or art consultants who may be able to broker the work to another client. In return for such services, the gallery, auctioneer, or broker will take a commission that can range from ten to forty percent, depending upon the work in question and the context. The more valuable a work, the more the owner is in the position to bargain for a lower commission. Keep in mind that you must sell the work for substantially more than you paid for it just to break even. This is because added-on commissions, transportation, and framing costs often mean that more is actually paid for the work than its agreed-upon value. As a result, it is more likely that you will end up losing your investment when reselling art, rather than gaining the tantalizing windfall profits discussed in the press. Therefore, buying art should be about the joy of possession and not just about the investment potential.

Regardless of how you sell art, there are some basic considerations to keep in mind. First, when you place the work with an agent, whether it be a gallery, auction house, or consultant, you are in effect consigning the work to them. What this means is that the agent is legally obligated to follow your instructions, must care for the work properly, and must account for any sales promptly and accurately. In consigning the work to an agent, you should be absolutely clear about the conditions of sale, the minimum price (called the reserve in an auction context), and the agent's commission. In calculating the minimum price, you should consider who will bear the expense of transporting the work to the buyer and the value of the frame, if relevant.

The second basic consideration is the consequences of capital gains tax. This is calculated upon the difference between the price originally paid for the work (which will be deemed zero if you or the gallery did not keep accurate records) and the amount received upon resale. Under current tax rates, you must turn over roughly a third of what you gained to Uncle Sam upon resale. Unfortunately, if you sell the work at a loss, it may be difficult to enjoy the benefits of a tax deduction unless you can claim to be a professional art investor, something that might be very difficult to do under current tax laws. Obviously you should consult your own tax accountant before undertaking any significant transactions involving potential tax consequences, as the tax laws are complex and often in the process of changing.

There are three main alternatives to resale in disposing of an artwork. The first is through trade. The gallery may be more apt to swap your piece for one it is trying to sell than to sell your work for you. The problem here is that you may not realize the full value of your work because the basis of a swap will likely be the dealer's appraisal measured against the asking price for the other piece of art. For example, if you have a work that a dealer says is worth five thousand dollars, and he or she offers you the opportunity to trade it for a work exhibited in the gallery that is also priced at five thousand dollars, this transaction may not be an even trade. First, you must make sure the "trade-in" price is accurate by having the artwork appraised by an independent dealer. Second, you must make sure that the work you are trading is discounted so that you are not assuming the entire cost of the dealer's commission. In other words, if your work is truly worth five thousand dollars, you should be able to trade it for a work exhibited in the seventy-five-hundred-dollar range. In order to make the trade, the dealer should offer you a healthy reduction in his or her typical fifty percent markup. Therefore, trading may offer convenience but not maximum value. The other two alternatives to resale follow.

Giving Art Away   The second alternative to selling your art is one that many people do (and sometimes inadvertently), leaving it to someone else through inheritance. Giving your art to family or friends is a time-honored way of controlling the ownership of your possessions after your physical demise. (The other way, leaving it to public institutions and the relevant tax considerations, is discussed below.) There are two basic ways to give art in this context. The first is to simply give it away in your lifetime to whomever you choose. This often makes sense, because under gift and estate tax, you can give up to ten thousand dollars a year per person without suffering adverse tax consequences. For such a gift to avoid current estate tax and inheritance law, it must have transpired more than two years prior to your death. If not, it is treated as part of your estate for tax purposes upon death.

The second way to give art to others is by directing such disposition to be carried out through your executor as directed in your will. If you die without a proper will (what's called intestate), your artwork, along with all your possessions, will be passed along to your family according to a formula that varies from state to state. For example, New York State does not recognize common-law marriage, so even if you live with someone all your adult life, but never formally married or wrote a will, your possessions will pass to your children, if any, or to your parents, if alive, or to brothers and sisters in descending order in relation to you. Therefore, your parents or some distant relative may end up with your possessions rather than the individual with whom you spent your life. This is why, among other reasons, it makes sense to create a valid binding will that sets forth how your possessions should be disposed of upon death.

This short book is not the place to go into the details of making a will, but there are several considerations unique to the disposition of artwork. The first concerns taxes. If you leave a valuable collection to someone of modest means, he or she will likely have to sell some of the work (often under adverse circumstances) to pay the inheritance tax owed. Estate planning should be considered if you want to leave the work intact to your loved ones. The second consideration is that your will must be specific as to your artwork. In other words, leaving the contents of your living room to Uncle Freddy and the contents of your bedroom to Aunt Sally will likely cause a fight between them over what work falls into these vague categories. Therefore the artwork should be named and left specifically to the person in question, and your will should be updated or codicils created to cover the expansion of your collection over time.

The third, and final, way to dispose of art is to give it to a charitable institution so that its appraised value can be used as a tax deduction. Unfortunately, under the new tax regulations that went into effect in the late eighties, such deductions are worth a good deal less than they once were. With the individual

Federal income-tax rate hovering somewhere between twenty-eight and thirty-three percent (depending on alternative minimum tax calculations), the value of your deduction is the same percentage, offset against your annual taxable income. In other words, the value of the deduction to offset ordinary income is roughly one-third of the appraised value.

Unfortunately, donating art can be as confusing and frustrating as trying to sell it. Once again, if you own top-value, prestigious art, curators will try to convince you to donate the work to their collections, but if you are a typical modest collector, it may be difficult to give it away. The reasons for donating art are often far more virtuous than realizing a tax advantage. Institutional museums and galleries are set up to store, preserve, and display art to an unmatched degree. You will fulfill your social obligations to maintain the integrity of the artwork to the fullest extent by placing it with a reputable museum or university collection.

Even if you place your work with a public collection, various questions remain. First and foremost is whether you can obligate the museum to keep and show the work. This can be difficult because museums are chronically short of storage space and in need of revenue. Therefore they tend to deaccession (i.e., sell) work in their collection to a far greater degree than commonly acknowledged to potential donors. A lesser consideration is whether or not the museum will preserve the integrity of a group of works within a single collection. Say, for instance, you amassed a unique collection of drawings by independent animators. It is the only such collection in the world, and it took you decades of hard work and loving care to put together. Therefore, you would like it to be kept and seen together, rather than sold off piecemeal to meet the museum's overhead or acquisition budget. Unfortunately, such conditions typically can be insisted upon only by the largest and wealthiest collectors, particularly those who give the museum an endowment along with the work.

Art As   Over the past quarter century, buying art has
Equity   become a respected way to invest money, and
              owning art has become an accepted sign of
              social prestige. Wealthy individuals, and
even large investment funds, have turned to art as a hedge against short-term economic losses. In an article entitled "Collecting: Hype and High Prices in the 80's," *The New York Times Magazine* explained the growing value of art as investment. "Changes in the U.S. tax laws . . . diminished the incentive to donate these works to museums, and their status as art made them seem more resistant to sudden economic slumps. . . . Institutions like Sotheby's and Citibank even started up art financing. . . . including a method by which the buyer can essentially take out a mortgage on a masterpiece."

In the same article, Richard H. Jenrette, chairman of the board of Equitable Life Assurance Society in New York, is quoted as saying, "The wolves of Wall Street have been buying a lot. . . . The same mentality that sees hidden assets in a company . . . will try to look for hidden value in an antiques collection. They approach it with the same attitude they would a takeover." This attitude has pumped vast amounts of money into the art market and has legitimized art as a form of investment. But, at the same time, it has inflated prices out of the reach of most individual collectors. Richard L. Feigen, a New York art dealer, recently was quoted elsewhere in *The New York Times*, with respect to the extension of credit for buying art, ". . . the problem is, there are regulations in the securities market that are not in the art market. By extending credit you are further inflating prices, which are rapidly getting out of control." Along the same lines, another dealer, Eugene V.

Thaw, was quoted in the same article as cautioning, ". . . it is not a conservative thing to do to lend money on art. It is the ethic of our time that is encouraging living out on the edge of credit."

The jury is still out on whether leveraging art purchases and collateralizing art to borrow money is good or bad for the art market. However, there are two aspects of this tendency that the beginning collector should keep in mind. First, the ability to take out a loan with an artwork as collateral is a wonderful justification for investing in art. It allows you to take advantage of the equity of your initial investment without forcing you to sell something that has become part of your life. On the other hand, buying art on a margin (i.e., with outside financing) inflates the price of art and therefore makes it difficult for the new collector to compete for the best art and antiquities. This is another reason why the collector must explore types of art outside the mainstream, in particular young artists whose style or subject matter may go against the grain of the typically conservative tastes of wealthy individuals and corporate collectors.

Specialization   Discussing the value of a collection as a whole leads to the final aspect of buying art that you should consider—specialization.

By focusing your purchases in defined areas you become an expert and therefore can make far more discriminating choices. This also gives you the opportunity to discover and monopolize a certain territory in which you will become known as a collector. If you buy only haphazardly or on a whim, you are more likely to end up with works you will not be happy with in years to come.

One of the great opportunities of collecting is to get to know a particular field and the artist and dealers who create it and keep it going. The most respected collectors are not necessarily the richest or most flamboyant but the most dedicated and

focused. In fact, with as little as a few thousand dollars a year, a smart, dedicated buyer can amass an impressive collection of art in less than a decade.

By avoiding the obvious, famous works of art and finding the proper balance between your desire and your financial and space limitations, you can develop a collection whose coherence and integrity will reflect well upon your intelligence and taste. Furthermore, as your collection grows, finding the right kind of art will become far easier. Dealers and artists will think of you first when the finest pieces become available. Finally you will become an integral part of the process that helps bring art into being, and that, more than any financial gain, is the highest value of buying and collecting art.

5 BUT IS IT ART?

The more you look at, and the more you buy, art, you will find that a good measure of greatness in art is its ability to embody many levels of appreciation. But some of it may appear too obscure or complex for the casual observer. Therefore, it will help if you know something about the history, social context, and theoretical foundations of contemporary art to develop an accurate sense of its value. Raymond Learsy, a well-known New York collector, has said: "As a collector you have to train your eye, your mind, and your perceptions. You have to understand what is important and what has come before, because nothing that is really significant in art just arrives there out of nowhere. . . . So I try to educate myself as much as I can to place myself where the artist was before he started painting that particular work of art. . . . Through my collecting, I try to distill an element of my time, to define the period in which I'm living by the art I'm collecting."

Ideas vs. Pictures For many people, contemporary art can be confusing, because, first, it frequently tends to be preoccupied with disposable Pop culture, and, at the same time, maddeningly obscure. In many ways these sometimes conflicting elements are a consequence of the visual power of the mass media supplanting many of the traditional functions of visual art. In other words, the media is now able to generate images on a scale and with the degree of effectiveness with which art cannot compete. Art, therefore, has been forced into a more marginal, reflective role and is less concerned with creating images than in manipulating existing imagery—much of it taken from popular culture—to highlight or to undermine its hidden effect on us. To understand, much less judge value in contemporary art, it is important to consider for a moment the deteriorating distinction between "fine" art and popular culture.

The key aspects of Pop culture, with respect to their influence upon fine art, have been: comics, rock music, advertising, film and television, and commercial design. These fungible goods, typically tossed away and ignored after their popularity wanes, have become the icons through which increasingly abstract and arcane visual artists anchor themselves to society. But whereas in the sixties the Pop artists used these icons largely in terms of their simple design elements or shock value, in the last decade artists began using Pop culture in a more fundamental and profound manner, questioning, among other issues, the definition of originality in an age of mass reproduction.

Examples of this later tendency range from "appropriation" artists who literally copy existing art and call the results their own, to artists who reposition existing ads and commercial objects into the art gallery context to suggest that culture (in both high and low forms of art) is based largely upon the simulation, rather than the representation, of nature.

One of the first artists to sense this upcoming change and use it in his art was Marcel Duchamp. By the mid-1920s he had thought through most of the important elements of twentieth-century art, in particular, the ideas of appropriating, or using, everyday objects or images to challenge accepted notions of art and social reality, and thinking of art as a form of language rather than as a means to reproduce nature. Jasper Johns and Andy Warhol were responsible for translating these ideas into an American idiom and for making them the foundation of American art over the past quarter century.

Therefore, instead of approaching contemporary art in the context of traditional connoisseurship (e.g., How skillful is the execution? What are the ideas behind the work? Is it derivative or original in both respects?), the beginning or new art buyer or collector needs a more subjective and conceptual strategy. For this it might be useful to consider three points made in a completely different medium, Wallace Stevens's poetic manifesto *Notes for a Supreme Fiction:* (1) It must be abstract; (2) It must change; and (3) It must give pleasure.

In the first instance, Stevens meant that art must be conscious of its own form and limited ability to represent nature and therefore be "abstract." He is not saying here that art should avoid recognizable imagery, but that such imagery should be handled in an ironic, sophisticated manner.

Stevens's second point ("It must change") means that art must be capable of multiple meanings that can shift, but not lose their potency, in a variety of contexts. A good example of this is the work of Andy Warhol, which, in spite of its apparent simplicity, is capable of provoking many different meanings to many different people. This keeps it alive and resistant to disposal.

Steven's third point ("It must give pleasure") is as obvious as it seems. Pleasure, like beauty, is in the eye of the beholder, so the purpose of this dictum is to encourage confidence in the beholder, *you*, the art buyer. The artwork must give *you* pleasure in a purely subjective and self-satisfying manner.

The point here is not to launch a generation of collectors walking through galleries muttering Stevens's three points as if they formed a mantra, but rather to demonstrate one approach that could help cut through superficial relationships to judge what may be of lasting value in contemporary art.

History or Hysteria? Although one must go beyond the status quo or accepted notions of value in art, it is still important for the newcomer to the art market to understand and be able to identify the basic art movements and the influential figures in those movements in order to follow what is being said in the magazines and exhibited in the galleries. Therefore what follows is a short listing and description of the key twentieth-century movements, their seminal personalities, and how they and their art served as precursors to much of the art that you will be looking at and buying today. Of course it must be stressed that this reductive overview is meant only as the simplest of guides to provide you with a foundation from which you can go beyond to develop your own sense of history and artistic value.

MAJOR MOVEMENTS IN
TWENTIETH-CENTURY PAINTING

I. Precursors to Modern Art

A. **Romanticism** Using color and gestural brush-strokes to evoke the artist's inner emotions. Example: Delacroix.

B. **Classicism** Stressing the formal elements of art through reference to classical compositions. Example: Ingres.

C. **Naturalism** Depicting everyday landscapes without allegorical or literary themes. Example: Corot.

D. Socialism Using art to represent and effect social conditions. Example: Courbet.

E. Primitivism Rhythmic designs and abstracted figures from the African, South American, Oriental colonies and trading partners of European empires. Examples: masks from Mali, woodblock prints from Japan, Tahitian totems.

F. Popular Culture American music, movies, and magazines expressing the freedom of European immigrants in America and the dynamics of African-American culture. Examples: movies, jazz, comics, industrial design, and architecture.

II. Modern Art (1860–1945)

A. Impressionism Combining everyday scenes with ironic references to the process of making art, both in reworking of traditional art themes and in making obvious the artist's brushstrokes. Examples: Manet, Monet, Degas, Cassatt.

B. Post-Impressionism Abstracting color and forms from their natural references to show the heightened psychological state of the artist. Examples: Van Gogh, Gauguin, Seurat, Cézanne.

C. Cubism Monochromatic breakdown of perspective into cubelike patterns. The handling of the picture plane changes from a window to look through to a flat wall to draw upon. Examples: Picasso, Braque.

D. Expressionism Using primitive or naive styles and intense color to express the neurotic, alienated aspect of art in the early twentieth century. Examples: Kirchner, Nolde, Munch.

E. Futurism Adding the element of motion to the Cubist's pseudo-mathematical organization of space. Example: Boccioni.

F. Dada Total break with traditional painting styles and themes; direct incorporation of everyday objects into art through collage and assemblage; stressing ideas or concepts over pictures or forms. Examples: Duchamp, Schwitters.

G. Constructivism Removing all natural reference to create an entirely new plastic language of art. Examples: Malevich, Mondrian.

H. Surrealism Enigmatic symbols (largely derived from pseudo-Freudian dreamwork) painted in an illustrational manner combined with Dada concepts of chance and spontaneity. Examples: De Chirico, Dali, Miró, Magritte.

I. Lyrical Modernism Using the stylistic and thematic breakthroughs of various vanguard movements to create a new sort of modern classicism. Examples: Matisse, Kandinsky, Picasso, Léger, Klee.

III. Post-Modernism (1945–Present)

A. Abstract Expressionism Isolating formal aspects of the painting process to express the artist's inner spiritual existence. Examples: Jackson Pollock, Willem de Kooning, Mark Rothko.

B. Post-Painterly Abstraction Anti-illusionistic art concerned only with the nonreferential aspects of painting: lines, color fields, squares, and cubes. Examples: Barnett Newman, Morris Louis, Ad Reinhardt, Frank Stella.

C. **Pop Art** Breaking with the traditional emphasis upon the artist's "hand" and abstract forms to incorporate vulgar aspects of pop culture into art. The first movement to comment upon the dislocation between images and reality in American society as a result of the mass media. Examples: Eduardo Paolozzi, Richard Hamilton, Andy Warhol, Roy Lichtenstein, Claes Oldenburg, H. C. Westermann, Ed Ruscha.

D. **Minimalism** Further purifying hard-edged abstraction to create art solely about its own material and processes. Examples: Donald Judd, Carl Andre, Robert Morris, Robert Ryman.

E. **Conceptualism** Using art to illustrate mental concepts, largely about the nature of reproduction or the function of art in society. Examples: Sol LeWitt, Jonathan Borofsky, Joseph Kosuth, Joseph Beuys.

F. **Earth Works** Applying conceptual ideas to monumental objects inserted into the real world. Examples: Robert Smithson, Michael Heizer, Walter DeMaria, Christo.

G. **Hyperrealism** Copying preexisting imagery (largely photographs) to show how the art of copying changes rather than imitates reality. Examples: Malcolm Morley, Chuck Close, Richard Estes.

H. **Neo-Expressionism** Turning expressionistic gestures into a formal language of art. Gestural brushstrokes, intense or gloomy colors, incongruous imagery, etc., are used to comment upon a tradition of art more than to bare the artist's inner soul. Examples: Julian Schnabel, Francesco Clemente, David Salle, Sigmar Polke, Susan Rothenberg, Elizabeth Murray, Anselm Kiefer, Pat Steir.

I. **Neo-Pop** Using vernacular styles as well as subjects to suggest how Pop culture has become the new American landscape. Examples: Keith Haring, Jean Michel Basquiat, Kenny Scharf, David Wojnarowicz, Barbara Kruger, Cindy Sherman, Gary Panter, Robert Longo.

J. **Neo-Geo** Undermining traditional notions of originality and representation in art by appropriating existing imagery from both fine art and consumer culture. Consequently, much of what would have been considered bad or meaningless in traditional terms—repetition, mistakes, vulgarity, utter banality, obscurity—is used to challenge accepted notions of good art and what makes an artist original. Examples: Sherrie Levine, Jeff Koons, Mike Bidlo, Richard Prince.

K. **Social Realism** Utilizing modern techniques and methods to point out political injustice and social inequality rather than to merely comment upon art itself. Examples: Leon Golub, Hans Haacke, Komar & Melamid, Jenny Holzer, Sue Coe.

Keep in mind that these art movements have little to do with the quality of any particular artwork. Movements are a form of shorthand that arise for the sake of convenience more than for accuracy. In fact, many of the names given to these movements began as terms of derision. Therefore, such names should only be used to help you distinguish between current philosophies and methods of art, most of which actually overlap and resist simple definition.

6 CONCLUSION

I n the interest of demystifying the process of buying art, this book has focused on the basic facts. In doing so the most obvious and important aspect of buying art has been left out—the pure simple fun of the endeavor. In some respects this seems so fundamental and obvious that it need not be stated, but in reaching a fervent rhetorical climax, this aspect of buying art needs to be raised to balance the information that has preceded it.

Once you have a sense of the terrain—the business, legal, and economic details laid out in this book—you must remember not to become bogged down by them. Buying art should not be guided by practical considerations only. The process of buying art is more like falling in love, and should be treated as such. A stroll through galleries or museums on a Saturday afternoon should be done for pleasure, not to prove intellectual or financial worth. Art is not just mental health food—it should allow you to get lost in pure, sensual abandonment. You should let the art take you over and carry your imagination beyond its ordinary limits. Of course when buying, rather than just enjoying, art, pleasure must be tempered with the practical considerations outlined here, but it is important to let your natural tendencies and temperament guide you rather than any sense of what others might think or tell you to do.

This book has tried to offer a neutral perspective that should compliment rather than limit or direct your own point of view. It suggests, however, that you look outside the obvious and easy things to buy in order to find the artwork that is meaningful and provocative to you. In so doing you will help to keep a broad spectrum of art alive in this country and will endow yourself with objects that have the power and beauty to improve the quality of your everyday life.

7 APPENDIX: FINDING ART/ FINDING OUT ABOUT ART

To begin to get a sense of what is going on in the art world and to help start you on your way, a brief and general listing of the major art galleries and museums across the country as well as the best books and magazines about art follows below.

New York Galleries

In most major cities across the United States, there are museums and galleries devoted to contemporary art. Nonetheless, New York continues to be the unavoidable center of the international art market. This is not to say you cannot find great art elsewhere, but, as the critic Clement Greenberg has written, "It's not necessary for an artist to be here (New York). It's as necessary for him as it has been ever since I've been around to show here. This is where reputations—larger reputations—are made or unmade." Even Douglas Cramer, a well-known West Coast collector, recently commented, "I will be killed by many of my West Coast friends and dealers for saying this, but I think New York is of great, great importance. I feel at this particular moment that New York offers the ultimate sanctification, the ultimate marketplace."

As was said earlier in the book, most New York galleries can be found in downtown SoHo or uptown along Fifty-seventh

Street, and they typically hang new shows each month, from September through June. Among galleries that show contemporary art, you can find both start-up shops that show work by largely unknown artists as well as established galleries, which exhibit work by modern masters that often ranges in price from thirty-five thousand to a hundred fifty thousand dollars and up for major painting and sculpture. It is relatively easy to get a sense of the established galleries—they are the ones whose artists seem to be written about the most and who take out prominent ads in art magazines each month. These galleries (listed alphabetically) and some of their major artists as of this writing comprise the following list.

Blum Helman. William Baziotes, Bryan Hunt, Ellsworth Kelly, Donald Sultan, Richard Tuttle.

Mary Boone. Ross Bleckner, Eric Fischl, Barbara Kruger, Brice Marden, Sigmar Polke, David Salle.

Leo Castelli. Richard Artschwager, Dan Flavin, Jasper Johns, Roy Lichtenstein, Claes Oldenburg, Robert Rauschenberg, James Rosenquist, Edward Ruscha, Richard Serra, Frank Stella.

Paula Cooper. Carl Andre, Jennifer Bartlett, Jonathan Borofsky, Donald Judd, Elizabeth Murray, Joel Shapiro.

André Emmerich. Anthony Caro, Burgoyne Diller, Al Held, David Hockney, Morris Louis, Kenneth Noland, Jules Olitski, Katherine Porter.

Marian Goodman. Marcel Broodthars, Tony Cragg, Martin Disler, Anselm Kiefer, Gerhard Richter.

Hirschl & Adler Modern. Joseph Beuys, Philip Pearlstein, Cy Twombly.

Sidney Janis. Oyvind Fahlstrom, Yves Klein, Duane Michals, George Segal, Tom Wesselmann.

M. Knoedler & Co. Richard Diebenkorn, Nancy Graves, Michael Heizer, Howard Hodgkin, Robert Motherwell, David Smith, Pat Steir.

Marlborough. Francis Bacon, Fernando Botero, Enzo Cucchi, Red Grooms, Alex Katz, R. B. Kitaj, Henry Moore, Larry Rivers.

Robert Miller. Diane Arbus, Louise Bourgeois, Jan Groover, Robert Mapplethorpe, McDermott & McGough, Joan Mitchell, Bruce Weber.

Pace Gallery. Jim Dine, Agnes Martin, Malcolm Morley, Lucas Samaras, Julian Schnabel, Saul Steinberg.

Pace/MacGill. Chuck Close, Robert Frank, Nan Goldin, Joel-Peter Witkin.

Sperone Westwater. Sandro Chia, Francesco Clemente, Enzo Cucchi, Susan Rothenberg.

John Weber. Alice Aycock, Hans Haacke, Sol LeWitt, Robert Smithson.

Unless you are buying prints, the galleries listed above show works by artists whose prices are generally out of the range of most new collectors, while the New York galleries listed below show work of similar quality but whose prices offer the new collector a more wide-ranging selection.

Brooke Alexander. John Ahearn, Richard Bosman, Jane Dickson, Tom Otterness, Judy Rifka, Robin Winters.

Josh Baer. Annette Lemieux, Nancy Spero.

Vrej Baghoomian. Jean Michel Basquiat, James Brown, George Condo.

Hal Bromm. Mike Bidlo, Luis Frangella, Krzysztof Wodiczko.

Diane Brown. Frederick Childs, Joel Fisher, Tony Oursler.

Ronald Feldman. Ida Applebroog, Arakawa, Chris Burden, Komar & Melamid, Mark Kostabi.

Frumkin/Adams. Robert Arneson, Luis Cruz Azaceta, Joan Brown, Roy DeForest, Peter Saul.

Galerie Lelong. Larry Bell, Walter De Maria, Robert Ryman.

Barbara Gladstone. Vito Acconci, Leon Golub, Jenny Holzer, Richard Prince.

Jay Gorney Modern Art. Sara Charlesworth, Peter Nagy, Tim Rollins + K.O.S., Haim Steinbach, Meyer Vaisman.

Gracie Mansion. Rodney Alan Greenblat, Stephen Lack, Gary Panter, David Sandlin, Rhonda Zwillinger.

Pat Hearn. Mary Heilmann, Ti Shan Hsu, Milan Kunc, Peter Schuyff, Philip Taaffe.

Phyllis Kind. Roger Brown, Robert Colescott, Duncan Hannah, Jim Nutt, Ed Paschke, Karl Wirsum.

Lennon, Weinberg. John Chamberlain, Chuck Connelly, H. C. Westermann.

Curt Marcus. Barbara Ess, Mark Innerst, Mark Tansey, Not Vital.

Metro Pictures. Mike Kelly, Robert Longo, Cindy Sherman, Laurie Simmons.

P.P.O.W. Paul Benny, Erika Rothenberg, Christy Rupp, David Wojnarowicz.

Max Protetch. Scott Burton, Judy Pfaff, William T. Wiley.

Tony Shafrazi. Donald Baechler, Keith Haring, Kenny Scharf.

Sharpe. Hanna Ahrens, Mark Dean, Jane Irish, Mark Strathy.

Holly Solomon. Nicholas Africano, Robert Kushner, Kim MacConnel, Nam June Paik, William Wegman.

Sonnabend. John Baldessari, Ashley Bickerton, Peter Halley, Jeff Koons.

Stux. Doug Anderson, Andreas Serrano, the Starn Twins.

The above sketch of key New York galleries is woefully limited because there are many other excellent galleries currently in New York, new ones opening all the time, and New York is not the only place in the world to see contemporary art. The above lists merely illustrate some of the most obvious places in New York to see and buy well-known contemporary art.

Major Galleries Outside New York With special arrangements made among gallery dealers, most galleries across the United States and in Europe show work of many of the same artists, or of similar quality, as those shown in New York. In addition, in each area you are likely to find galleries that specialize in the work of local or regional artists. As a general rule, the best place to find a listing of galleries is in a publication called *Gallery Guide*, which publishes monthly listings of shows in editions devoted to several U.S. cities. The *Guide* can be found on newsstands, is given away free in galleries, or can be subscribed to. Gallery listings also can almost always be found in a city's Sunday newspaper or in the national or local art magazines, where galleries advertise their shows each month. For directories that list galleries across the United States, you can consult the annual guides to galleries published by *Art in America* and *Art News* magazines, both of which provide an exhaustive list of galleries, addresses, and names of artists each gallery shows.

Having said the above, it seems logical to point out that outside New York, the two principal cities with unusually active contemporary art scenes and markets are Los Angeles and Chicago. What follows, then, is a short and selected list of key galleries in the Los Angeles and Chicago areas associated with contemporary artists in particular.

Los Angeles Area Galleries

Asher/Faure
Dennis Anderson
Jan Baum
Marilyn Butler
Cirrus
Rosamund Felsen

Fred Hoffman
Gemini G.E.L.
L.A. Louver
Margo Leavin
Luhring Augustine Hetzler
Daniel Weinberg

Chicago Area Galleries

Dart
Richard Gray
Rhona Hoffman
Hokin/Kaufman

Phyllis Kind
Randolph Street
Betsy Rosenfield
Struve
Donald Young

Museums and Alternative Spaces Other than in galleries and museums, alternative spaces are the best places to get a sense of what is happening in the art world. The single most influential museum event in the contemporary American art market is the Whitney Museum of American Art Biennial Exhibition. The Biennial ostensibly brings together the best art made in America in the previous two years and tends to bolster and reflect mainstream values. However, if you don't treat the exhibition as gospel, it provides a useful barometer of mainstream tendencies and an opportunity to judge a range of recent artwork bumped up against each other in an institutional context. Some of the key museums across the United States include:

Albright-Knox Art Gallery (Buffalo, New York)

The Aldrich Museum of Contemporary Art (Ridgefield, Connecticut)
Art Institute of Chicago
The Brooklyn Museum (Brooklyn, New York)
Dallas Museum of Art
The Detroit Institute of Arts
Dia Art Foundation (New York City)
The Solomon R. Guggenheim Museum (New York City)
Hirshhorn Museum and Sculpture Garden, Smithsonian Institution (Washington, D.C.)
Illinois State University Art Galleries (Normal, Illinois)
Institute of Contemporary Art (Boston)
Kimbell Art Museum (Fort Worth, Texas)
La Jolla Museum of Contemporary Art (La Jolla, California)
Los Angeles County Museum of Art
The Menil Collection (Houston, Texas)
The Metropolitan Museum of Art (New York City)
The Minneapolis Institute of Arts
The Museum of Contemporary Art (Los Angeles)
Museum of Fine Arts (Boston)
The Museum of Modern Art (New York City)
National Museum of American Art, Smithsonian Institution (Washington, D.C.)
Nelson-Atkins Museum of Art (Kansas City, Missouri)
Neuberger Museum, State University of New York (Purchase, New York)
Philadelphia Museum of Art
The Phillips Collection (Washington, D.C.)
San Francisco Museum of Modern Art
Storm King Art Center (Mountainville, New York)
Wadsworth Atheneum (Hartford, Connecticut)
Walker Art Center (Minneapolis)
Yale University Art Gallery (New Haven, Connecticut)

In addition, small university galleries and alternative spaces provide the arena for art that frequently makes it into the mainstream institutions listed above. For example, Hallswalls, associated with The State University of New York in Buffalo, New York, spawned a surprising number of well-known contemporary artists already mentioned, Robert Longo and Cindy Sherman among them. Other important alternative spaces across the country include:

Artists Space (New York City)
City Without Walls (Newark, New Jersey)
Diverse Works (Houston, Texas)
Franklin Furnace (New York City)
Institute for Contemporary Art, P.S. 1 Museum (Long Island City, New York)
INTAR Latin American Gallery (New York City)
LACE (Los Angeles)
N.A.M.E. Gallery (Chicago)
The New Museum of Contemporary Art (New York City)
Nexus Contemporary Art Center (Atlanta, Georgia)
Real Art Ways (Hartford, Connecticut)

Magazines There are three main types of publications from which you can glean a sense of what is happening in the art world: glossy specialty magazines, academic journals, and general publications with features and/or sections devoted to visual art.

Specialty Magazines There are a number of well-known art magazines that you can look to for information and entertainment. Virtually all of them are valuable for the ads that announce the major shows each month and the reviews that assess the shows advertised a month or so before. Over the past decade, *Artforum* has been the most influential art magazine, although for the newcomer to the art world, its articles may at times be too specialized, with hard-going art-critical and theoretical content. *Art in America* and *Arts* magazines, also monthly, mix scholarly articles and essays about the current art scene. *Art News* is slanted toward art reportage and artist profiles, while *Flash Art* has a recognizable international perspective. Few, if any, people read all of these magazines each month. Most who follow the art world choose one or two of the magazines to get a random sample of what is out there and then go to the other publications for specific articles and reviews of work of particular interest. In addition, there are specialty magazines, like *Artscribe* or *Connoisseur*, devoted to a relatively narrow aspect of the art world, rather than a broad overview of the contemporary scene.

Academic Journals As the name implies, academic journals are not geared to the average collector, but they have proven to be fertile ground for those who wish to go beyond the often trendy art journals. Of the academic journals, two radically different ones are of note. The *College Art Journal* is the classic place where professors publish so as not to perish. The language can be difficult, but each issue contains noteworthy articles by art professors who fight on the front lines of cultural literacy. *October* is academic in tone, but not in affiliation. It is the most important publication for the critics who have propelled recent art into the forefront of philosophical theory.

General Publications Virtually every daily, weekly, and monthly general-interest newspaper or magazine contains art reviews. Three of the most influential sources of popular opinion about the arts are *The New York Times*, *The New*

Yorker, and *Time* magazine. When an artist is recognized in these highly regarded mainstream publications, careers are made. This has been true since *Life* magazine featured Jackson Pollock in the fifties, turning him from an obscure artist into a cultural icon. A few years later, in 1955, *Time* magazine launched Jasper Johns's career with a feature on the then twenty-five-year-old artist. Today collectors, curators, and other artists still look to these media institutions for a consensus on who are the great artists of our time. Unfortunately, this kind of coverage can also lead to the same well-known artists being mentioned over and over again. For broader coverage—of interesting and up-to-the-minute cutting-edge figures—there are excellent journals and magazines, some local, some with a more limited national distribution, published independently of the major news and magazine organizations and spawning a new generation of art writers that should not be overlooked.

Books   In addition to reading the art magazines and the reviews in national magazines and local dailies, there are a number of books that are useful to read to get a sense of the context in which contemporary art is being made.

- For a good overview of modern art as a whole, the following books provide useful surveys: Norbert Lynton, *The Story of Modern Art* (New York: Phaidon); Werner Haftmann, *Painting in the Twentieth Century* (New York: Praeger); John Russell, *The Meanings of Modern Art* (New York: Harper & Row).

- For an overview of what was considered the best art of the last decade, you might want to read: *New Art* (New York:

Harry N. Abrams), a large format, pictures-only compendium; Jerry Saltz, *Beyond Boundaries: New York's New Art* (New York: A. Van der Marck Editions); Howard Singerman, ed., *Individuals: A Selected History of Contemporary Art* (New York: Abbeville), the catalogue to one of the most important West Coast art exhibitions of the decade.

- Some of the best compilations of writings and illustrations that have helped to set the tone for art in the last decade (and may help explain it to you) include: Yves-Alain Bois et al., *Endgame: Reference and Simulation in Recent Painting and Sculpture* (Cambridge: MIT Press); Brian Wallis, ed., *Art After Modernism* (New York: The New Museum of Contemporary Art); Brian Wallis, ed., *Modern Dreams* (Cambridge: MIT Press); Paul Taylor, ed., *Post-Pop Art* (Cambridge: MIT Press); Hal Foster, ed., *The Anti-Aesthetic: Essays on Postmodern Culture* (Port Townsend, Washington: The Bay Press).

- The compilations listed above include most of the influential essays that have served as the manifestos of various movements in recent American art. Some of the books by these important philosophers and writers are as follows: Jean Baudrillard, *Simulations* (New York: Semiotext(e)); Walter Benjamin, *Illuminations* (New York: Schocken Books); Guy DeBord, *Society of the Spectacle* (Detroit: Black and Red Press); Paul DeMan, *Allegories of Reading* (New Haven: Yale University Press); Jacques Derrida, *The Parergon* (Baltimore: Johns Hopkins University Press); Michel Foucault, *The Order of Things* (New York: Vintage Books); Frederic Jameson, *The Political Unconsciousness* (Ithaca: Cornell University Press); Jean-Francois Lyotard, *Driftworks* (New York: Semiotext(e)).

- Finally, for more information regarding the legal issues involved in buying and owning art, the following three books provide an invaluable source of reference: Tad Crawford, *Legal Guide for the Visual Artist* (New York: Madison Square Press); Franklin Feldman and Stephen E. Weil, with Susan Duke Biederman, *Art Law* (Boston: Little, Brown and Company); John Henry Merryman and Albert E. Elsen, *Law, Ethics and the Visual Arts* (Philadelphia: University of Pennsylvania).

TV or Not TV Throughout the history of Western art, its availability to the public has been made possible through the kinds of sources and media listed in this Appendix. You can see art by visiting galleries or museums or by reading publications that reproduce art or reduce it to writing. The principal change from 1500 to 1900 was that industrialists replaced aristocrats as the principal patrons of the arts. Similarly, art became more public and more concerned about real conditions, and artists became more committed to expressing their own concerns rather than those of church or state.

In our own lifetime, however, a new way to see art has emerged. Through television, art is now disseminated in a more tangible way to a greater number of people than ever before. At the same time, the rise of visual over verbal literacy in our culture has given art ever greater social impact. Art on television and art in fashion and design have become an important barometer of cultural influence and value and have catapulted the artist into celebrity status.

Through independent documentaries on PBS, videos produced by museums in conjunction with blockbuster exhibitions, and occasional news features, the medium of television is now able to provide wonderful insights into artists, which beforehand you could only get by knowing the artist personally. Therefore, more and more, people have become familiar with artists through television or, even, through movies rather than in print. Signs of ultimate artistic success consist now as much in being the backdrop for feature films like *Legal Eagles*, *Down and Out in Beverly Hills*, or *Wall Street*, as in being featured in *The New York Times Magazine*. For now, this phenomenon can have the effect of bolstering the dominance of the new over the good in contemporary art, but there are signs that in the near future the marriage of video and computer technology will revolutionize our ability to see and purchase art. For instance, laser discs can now store up to thirty thousand single images with amazing clarity and detail (particularly when used in conjunction with high-definition television). Computer networks linked by optical fibers allow images stored in one place to be instantly transmitted to another. Within a decade many art galleries will store images by their artists that you will be able to access from anywhere in the country. As a result, someone in a beach house in Malibu could peruse every gallery in SoHo in an hour or two without ever leaving home. Further, purchases could be made over the phone, with the bill of sale faxed back and forth. Similarly, you may be able to look through museum exhibitions and collections on video for a modest access fee. Intelligent digital documentation used as a supplement to viewing the art object itself undoubtedly will further the importance of visual art in American culture in the years to come as it also serves to stimulate its financial value.